Last Minute

Weddings

D1405764

By
Donna A. Bankhead
and
Lynnette Blas

CAREER PRESS

Franklin Lakes, NJ

LAST MINUTE WEDDINGS
Cover design by Foster & Foster
Printed in the U.S.A. by Book-mart Press

To order this title, please call toll-free 1-800-CAREER-1 (NJ and Canada: 201-848-0310) to order using VISA or Master Card, or for further information on books from Career Press.

The Career Press, Inc., 3 Tice Road, PO Box 687, Franklin Lakes, NJ 07417

Library of Congress Cataloging-in-Publication Data

Bankhead, Donna A.
    Last minute weddings / by Donna A. Bankhead and Lynnette Blas.
        p.   cm.
    Includes index.
    ISBN 1-56414-415-1 (pbk.)
        1. Weddings—United States—Planning. 2. Wedding etiquette-
-United States.   3. Marriage customs and rites—United States.
    1. Blas, Lynnette. II. Title.
HQ745.B36   1999   395
395.2'2—dc21   BAN   99-22503
                                                            CIP

To Bill, Emily, Chance, and Abby. —D.A.B.
To Paul. —L.B.

Acknowledgments

This book would never have gotten off the ground if it weren't for the help and encouragement of a multitude of people. We would like to thank Dr. Peter Wollheim for his sound advice and unwavering enthusiasm from the day we got the idea for the book until we put the manuscript in the mail. Special thanks go out to Kent Anderson for pointing us in the right direction and to the staff at Odyssey Tour & Travel in Dallas for their above-and-beyond support. We also thank the wedding service providers across the country who patiently answered all of our questions and eagerly provided their insight on organizing a last minute wedding. And finally, we owe a huge debt of gratitude to our families for putting up with us as we burned the midnight oil and hogged the phones, fax machines, and computers.

 *Contents*

 *Introduction*

It's happened. You've searched and waited your whole life and now you've found your soul mate—the person who makes your life worth living, the one you'll share your love, hopes, dreams, and secrets with until the end of time. You've discovered your destiny. So why put that destiny on hold for a year or two while you plan your wedding? It's not necessary.

Contrary to popular belief, it *is* possible to plan a terrific wedding—one with all the beauty, joy, and magic you've always dreamed of—in just a few short months. In fact, last minute weddings—those that are put together in six months or less—are becoming increasingly common in the hectic, speed-of-light society we live in today. Time has become a precious commodity and many couples are opting to spend considerably less of it organizing a wedding. Many face pressures from work, school, and family and wouldn't dream of tying up a year arranging a wedding. For others, circumstances, such as an upcoming job transfer, military service, or ill health of a family member, dictate a cutback in the amount of planning time available. Still others would rather cut to the chase and *be* married than spend a whole year planning to *get* married.

Believe it or not, planning a wedding at the last minute can be easier and less stressful than taking a year or

Last Minute Weddings

more to pull one together. It forces you to focus on what's really important to you—what you *truly* want for your special day—and push aside all of the extraneous details that some magazine says you absolutely *must* have if you're going to put on a respectable wedding. And because you have a limited amount of time, you make your decisions and move on. No hemming and hawing, no "maybe mauve would look better than dusty rose," no changing your mind so often you forget what you're deciding about. You go with your gut and that's that.

Still, planning even a quick wedding can seem like an overwhelming task. That's where this book comes in. You'll find everything you need to know to streamline preparations and make your last minute wedding come off without a hitch. From deciding on the Big Four (the date, place, budget, and wedding party) to providing the frills, such as wedding programs and bridal birdseed, we've got you covered. Tasks are discussed in descending order from the ones you absolutely must tackle first to the ones you can afford to put off until the eleventh hour or skip altogether. You'll also find advice about some of the things on the periphery of the wedding, things like picking out the rings, planning the honeymoon, and enjoying prewedding festivities and showers.

If a big wedding is just not your style, then Chapter 6 is written especially for you. In this section, you'll learn how to pull off the ultimate in last minute weddings— eloping. It covers the pros and cons of eloping, how to choose a time and place to get married, where to find out about marriage license requirements, what to wear, even how to announce your marriage and throw a reception when you return home.

You'll also find lots of tips for keeping the cost down. Planning a last minute wedding can cost more than others because many merchants charge a premium price if you ask them to hurry. If you're on a budget, look for these cost-cutting suggestions.

Finally, you'll find the workhorse of this book—the Appendices. While the chapters are packed with great advice and ideas on planning your last minute wedding, the Appendices give you the nuts-and-bolts information you'll need to pull it off. You'll find names and addresses of vendors who specialize in providing quality wedding supplies, things like invitations, favors, mementos, attendants' gifts, cake toppers, and decorations, in a hurry and at a fair price. Other resources that will be invaluable in your planning, such as addresses for helpful Web sites, are also included. And to help you stay organized, you'll find a timeline and wedding planning worksheets. If you're thinking elopement is the way to go, check out the listing of wedding chapels and wedding service providers across the country that cater to couples who want to get married on the fly.

Getting to the altar in style doesn't have to be a white-knuckled, exhausting marathon that leaves you yearning for a damp cloth and a dark room. With help from *Last Minute Weddings*, your wedding can be a fun, manageable, and delightfully short sprint across the finish line.

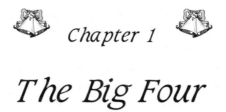

Chapter 1

The Big Four

Not long ago, I ran into a young woman in a bookstore. I mean, I literally ran into her. She was huddled cross-legged on the floor over an entire library of wedding-planning books. On her lap and strewn all around her were stacks of books she had pulled off the shelves. Her face, as she looked up at me when I tripped over her, had the same stricken expression Wiley Coyote gets right before a boulder lands on his head. She apologized for blocking the aisle and then blurted out, practically in tears, "I'm getting married in three months and it's just so overwhelming!" She explained that all of the books she had looked at told her she couldn't possibly expect to pull off a decent wedding in less than a year, what with the designer dress, engraved invitations, and hand-dipped chocolates she would *surely* want to have. As she slumped there on the floor and poured out her frustration, it was clear that planning the ceremony that would unite her with the love of her life was going to be far more painful than being stomped on in a bookstore.

Most brides-to-be experience, to some degree, the panic that the young woman in the bookstore felt as they try to figure out how to begin planning their wedding. Throw in the complication of an abbreviated engagement period—

and consequently, a shortened amount of time for organizing increases exponentially.

It truly doesn't have to be that way. Whether you've got six months or six weeks, you can pull off a terrific wedding without pulling out all of your hair. You can actually enjoy the process of organizing this ceremony that will change your life.

But before you call a single florist or try on your first wedding gown, find yourself a quiet corner, pour a cup of whatever it is you like to drink, and read this book. It will help you lay the foundation for an enjoyable planning process by putting things into perspective and setting some ground rules.

Keep in mind that this is *your* wedding. It's not your mother's, sister's, mother-in-law's, or friend's. Plan it the way you want it. You can listen to the advice of others and accept help if you like, but take and keep control of the decision-making from the very start.

The Big Four

The most important wedding decisions you'll have to make (aside from who you'll marry, of course) involve what we call the Big Four: 1) picking the date, 2) setting the budget, 3) choosing wedding and reception locations, and 4) selecting members of the wedding party. While they're separate issues you'll have to consider individually, the Big Four are intertwined; each can affect your decision about the others. For example, let's say you want your best friend, Karen, to be in the wedding, but she'll be right in the middle of final exams on the day you've chosen to get married. You could change the date, but the church you've wanted to get married in since you were a little girl is booked solid for months after that. Because you're a member of the church, using it would be free; a change in location could jack your costs up by hundreds, even thousands, of dollars. So what do you do?

This one hitch in selecting your wedding party affects the other three factors of date, location, and budget, and makes the difficulty of pulling the Big Four together on a tight schedule all the more difficult.

Because this is bound to happen, you have to be flexible and willing to consider several alternative scenarios in the early planning stages. Begin by prioritizing the Big Four: Which of the four is the most important to you and your future mate? Using the example above, let's say the location is your top priority but you still would like your friend to be your maid of honor. Try tweaking the date a bit. The church may be booked every weekend for the next few months, but what about weeknights? Would you be willing to get married on, say, a Thursday evening a week after Karen's finals are over? Or maybe the date is etched in stone and can't be changed. If Karen had enough notice to prepare for her finals early, could she fly in for the weekend or just the wedding day? With a little creativity, you'll be able to adjust the date, budget, place, and people until you find the mix that will work for you.

Picking the Date

Although you have to pick the date before you can start making any plans for the ceremony and reception, give some thought to the type of wedding you want as you sit down with the calendar. Do you dream of a swirling-clouds-of-lace Cinderella wedding? Then you'd better have more than a week or two to make the arrangements. For an elaborate affair with all (or most of) the trimmings, allow at least two months. Even better—three to six months of planning time will give you a little wiggle room.

On the other hand, if time is of the essence or you're just not the Cinderella-wedding type, in less than a month's time you can plan a small, simple wedding ceremony and reception that will be just as lovely and meaningful as a grand affair.

Another factor to consider when choosing the date for a last minute wedding is your out-of-town guests. Very few people can afford to pay undiscounted airfares, so try to give at least a few weeks' notice if you have family and/or friends who'll need to fly in or make arrangements for lodging.

A third factor in choosing your date is the availability of wedding service vendors, such as caterers, florists, and photographers. Peak wedding months are May through October. Holidays like Christmas, Valentine's Day, and even April Fool's Day are also very popular. If you're planning on a tight schedule *and* your date falls within one of the peak times, your options are going to be more limited and you may have to make more compromises than if your wedding date were in a less-busy period. Instead of a full meal, for example, you may have to settle for a light hors d'oeuvre buffet in order for the caterer to squeeze you in between the six other weddings that were booked last year for that same day.

When time is tight you might consider hiring a wedding consultant to help you with arranging the details of your wedding. Consultants who have worked in your town for a while will know the best vendors to call for your specific needs and will have resources and knowledge that will be invaluable in planning your wedding. They may tack on an additional fee for planning your wedding in such a short amount of time, but the stress and hair-pulling they'll save you may be worth it.

Peak wedding periods not only affect the availability of wedding vendors, they also determine how much you're going to fork out for their services. Which leads us to number two of the Big Four: setting a budget.

Setting a Budget

If you're planning a sky-is-the-limit affair and don't care what it costs, budget isn't one of your concerns right now. Go out and have a ball putting together your wedding celebration. But if there is a bottom to your pockets, it's imperative that you set a budget right from the start. The average wedding costs around $20,000, but many, many couples (and their families) spend far less than that. Becky, the mother of five now-grown children, helped each of her children, (three of whom are girls) plan their weddings. She never spent more than $3,000 on any of these nuptial celebrations, which were all large and ranged from a very formal, proper affair to a casual, blue-jeans event.

Think clearly and realistically about how much you can (and want to) spend *before* you sit down with the florist, photographer, or any other vendor. You can go through an awful lot of money very quickly if you make impulsive decisions without clearly defined and well-thought-out budgetary parameters. If family members are picking up some or all of your wedding expenses, they need to be in on the budget discussions as well. Find out how much they're willing to contribute and who will be paying for what. Mapping out who pays for what right in the beginning will eliminate many misunderstandings down the line.

After you've decided how much you will spend, prioritize your list of wedding wants. What is the single most important thing that you want in your wedding? A drop-dead gorgeous gown? A huge, no-holds-barred reception with a seven-course meal prepared by the finest chef in town? Decorations they'll be talking about for years to come? Get an idea of how much your must-have item will cost, then see what's left. If there's barely enough to buy your garter, you might want to rethink the must-have item or figure out a way to scale it back.

Scaling back doesn't necessarily mean settling for second rate—it means being smart and taking advantage of opportunities you may not have thought about before. For example, if you, your fiancé, or either set of parents is a member of a religious organization, you may be able to use its facilities for free or at a discount. Also, decorations can be significantly less expensive when you or a creative friend make and arrange them.

Remember that along with the big-ticket items—the dress, the photographer, the reception—you're going to have a lot of little expenses to deal with also. Things like thank you notes and postage, the marriage license, and gifts for the attendants add up quickly and can be budget busters if you don't plan for them. And the money for your wedding rings and the honeymoon has to come from somewhere, so budget for those as well. Take a look at the Wedding Timeline in Appendix A. It will give you a good idea of all the things you'll pay for before you say, "I do."

Choosing Your Location

Common wedding and reception locations, such as churches, temples, halls, and hotels, book up quickly for the peak wedding months. These places also tend to be hard to get on short notice during the holiday season because they have more holiday-related activities, parties, and events. But for the determined last minute wedding planner, there are ways to work around these obstacles.

Last Minute Weddings

Obviously, Saturdays during peak months and holiday seasons are going to be next to impossible to book on short notice unless you happen to be in the right place at the right time when someone cancels a reservation at the last minute. But if you're willing to have your ceremony on a weeknight or a nontraditional time of day, your range of options widens significantly. For example, a chapel booked on a Saturday evening may be available that morning for an early wedding and brunch reception. You can even increase your odds of finding an open date at a hotel or hall if you can have your wedding on a Friday night or a Sunday.

There's no rule that says you have to get married in a common wedding setting. In your search for the perfect location, don't overlook the not-so-standard places your hometown and surrounding areas have to offer. Is there a tourist attraction nearby that would make for a unique wedding/reception site? At Rock City outside of Chattanooga, Tenn., for example, you can hold a private affair on a grassy bluff overlooking a fabulous view that goes on forever. Gold Canyon, Ariz., has a movie ranch, complete with boardwalks, saloon, horses and buggies, and a hall that can accommodate weddings and receptions. Wineries and nature parks offer spectacular scenery and often have facilities to rent. Dude ranches, ski lodges, golf courses, historic buildings, and public parks are all possibilities.

An exciting alternate wedding site is on a cruise liner. For a cruise wedding, you'll need to make reservations about six months out, but you may find an opening in less time than that, especially during low season. (High and low seasons vary depending on the location, so contact a travel agent for information on specific areas.) For an additional price, cruise lines offer packages that include flowers, cake, photography, and many other amenities of a traditional wedding. Some lines allow the wedding party and guests to board the ship several hours before sailing to witness the nuptials and enjoy the reception. Guests disembark before the ship sets sail, and the newlyweds are on their own to enjoy their honeymoon cruise alone. Other lines prohibit anyone but passengers from boarding the ship, so you should definitely work with a travel agent to get specifics and make arrangements for a cruise wedding.

When you check out alternative wedding/reception sites, be sure to ask about a few important details before you make a commitment. First, what is the policy on food? Are you required to use in-house caterers? If you're planning to have your mom and Aunt Opal do all the cooking for the reception, ask if you can bring food in.

Second, who is responsible for cleanup? Typically, a hall or hotel will include cleanup in the rental cost. However, if you opt for a nontraditional wedding site, such as a public park, you may be responsible for cleaning up. In that case, you'll either have to find volunteers for the job or hire a professional cleaning service to take care of it.

Third, does the location have any decorations that you can use free of charge? Many places allow wedding parties to borrow any candelabras, decorative plants, or seasonal wedding arrangements they may have. If these will work with your decorating scheme, you can use them, and shave a few dollars off of your expenses as well.

Selecting the Wedding Party

Twenty years ago, selecting members of the wedding party was relatively easy: The bride chose her best girlfriends and sisters to stand up for her and the groom asked his brothers and male friends. Now, between co-ed college dorms, men and women teaming up in the office, and the virtual extinction of female-only or male-only

Last Minute Weddings

professions, it's not at all uncommon for people to have close friends of both genders. If this is your situation, don't feel uncomfortable or weird about having your male friend(s) stand up for you or your fiancé's female friend(s) stand up for him. Even mixed-gender maids/matrons of honor and best men are becoming more and more common all the time. In your program (should you choose to have one) you can simply list them as honor attendants.

Typically, the same number of attendants stand up for each the bride and groom. (Keep in mind that the greater the number of attendants, the more you'll need to budget for things like flowers, photographs, and gifts.) The honor of attendant should be given to those with whom you and/or your groom (or bride) have a close and special relationship, not to someone you simply feel obligated to include in the festivities. And because these people are special to you, you should consider their needs before you rush to the phone and ask them to be in your last minute wedding.

Regardless of whom you ask to stand up for you, make sure you give them plenty of time to make their travel and lodging arrangements. Also, although it's hard to imagine anything could be as important as your wedding, be aware of upcoming events in their lives as well as your own. It's a pretty safe bet that if you ask your old college roommate to be in your wedding, which just happens to fall on the day she's due to deliver her sextuplets, she won't be able to accept the honor.

Another consideration when choosing attendants is finances. Being in someone else's wedding can be an expensive proposition. The dress or tuxedo, travel and lodging expenses, and all the other things add up quickly. If your fiancé's best friend is in the midst of filing for bankruptcy, he may not welcome the opportunity to burrow deeper into debt just to be in your wedding—especially with very little time to save and plan. If your budget allows it and it's very important to you that someone with financial difficulties be in your wedding, you might offer to foot the bill.

In addition to attendants, think about any other people you'd like to include in the wedding party. What about a flower girl and/or ring bearer? Consider the age and temperament of any kids you're thinking of asking to be in the ceremony. While a bit of childlike behavior—such as dropping the ring pillow or giggling during the kiss—can be cute, a sugar-crazed demon who trips the bridesmaids or moons the audience from the altar can have you gritting your teeth in anger. You might laugh about it in years to come, but you definitely won't see the humor in this behavior in the middle of the ceremony.

Another member of the wedding party to consider is the person who will walk the bride down the aisle. Fifty years ago, the choice was a no-brainer—the father of the bride was given the honor. Now, with blended families, single-parent households, and an infinite number of other family structures, the choice isn't always that easy anymore.

This can be one of the stickier issues in planning a wedding. Natural substitutes for an absent father can be a brother, grandfather, uncle, or close male friend. But what if the bride is close to both father and stepfather? Or if the bride saw her father occasionally while growing up but never had much of a relationship with him?

Although there's not a single one-size-fits-all answer, other brides have found some creative ways to resolve the problem. For example, Mindy was close to her father and stepfather and wanted to include both in her wedding. Her solution was to have her stepfather walk her halfway down the aisle, where her natural father was waiting to escort her the rest of the way. Having a father on one arm and stepfather on the other is another possible solution to this dilemma, provided the two men can be civil toward each other and the aisle is wide enough to accommodate three people.

In the case of a father who's never played a meaningful role in the bride's life, no one says he has to be included in the ceremony. Another man could substitute, but it's becoming more common in cases like this for the bride's mother to be the escort or for the bride to make the trek by herself.

There are no laws that cover this issue. Do what you feel is best for your situation. Talk with friends who've been in the same situation or post your questions on one of the many bridal/wedding chat rooms or bulletin boards on the Internet. (See Appendix B.) You'll get advice and opinions from people across the country who've been there and done that.

Deciding on and coordinating the Big Four at short notice can be a daunting task, but after they're taken care of, the hard part's over. You'll still be busy with the rest of your planning, but you're finished with the really big decisions. Just keep in mind that this grand event you're putting together is a celebration in which you and your beloved are the main attraction. Relax, keep your sense of humor, and enjoy this very special time in your life.

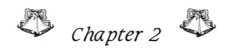

Chapter 2

The Must-haves

The must-haves are the officiant, marriage license, wedding dress, and photographer. These are every bit as important in planning your wedding as the Big Four. Unlike the Big Four, however, each is independent of the others. In other words, your choice of photographer won't impact when you'll get your marriage license or who will officiate the wedding. Although you may have to spend a good deal of time taking care of some of the must-haves (put them somewhere near the top of your list), they won't be nearly as complicated to orchestrate as the Big Four.

The Officiant

In most states, marriages can be legally performed by ministers, priests, rabbis, and other clergy members; current and retired judges; and officials such as the governor, lieutenant governor, and city mayor. To find out who can officiate weddings in your state, call the number listed under *Marriage Licenses* in the county government pages of your phone book.

Your search for an officiant may be short and sweet if you're being married in a religious setting where you are a practicing member. Before you make any commitments, though, be sure you feel comfortable with the officiant and his or her requirements. For example, you and your future spouse may be required to participate in premarital counseling before you can be pronounced husband and wife (and you may not have time for that!). Also, if you want someone other than a house cleric to perform the ceremony or the staff music director to handle the music, you'll need to obtain special permission well in advance.

Even if you're not marrying in a religious setting, you can still have a religious ceremony. Ask your minister, priest, rabbi, or other clergy if he or she is willing to perform weddings in other locations such as your yard or a park. If not, check your yellow pages under *Wedding Chapels and Ceremonies*. It's very likely you'll find listings for several clergy members who will marry you any time, any place.

For a civil ceremony, call your county offices for information about locating a judge who can officiate. The yellow pages may also list some other people who are willing and able to perform civil ceremonies.

When you interview potential officiants, be sure to tell them the type of wedding you're planning. Some religious officiants who are accustomed to performing formal ceremonies may not feel comfortable presiding over your casual backyard wedding. Likewise, a Justice of the Peace who is used to short-and-sweet lunch-break weddings may not be up to waxing eloquently for your formal ceremony.

The Marriage License

Marriage license requirements vary from state to state. Some states issue licenses that are valid only in the county where they're purchased; others require medical examinations or a waiting period; and some mandate that both the bride and groom apply for the license in person. To find the requirements in your area, contact your county offices or look under *Marriage Licenses* in the county government pages of your phone book.

Regardless of how simple the requirements in your state are, don't put off getting your marriage license until the very last minute. Imagine the heart palpitations you'll experience if you go to the county office on the day before your wedding only to find that the office is closed while they set up their computer network. Get your license as far ahead of time as you can—it'll be one less eleventh-hour detail you'll have to worry about.

The Wedding Dress

Shopping for your wedding dress can start out as one of the most exciting parts of planning a wedding but then quickly turn into one of the most frustrating. You're going to be especially vulnerable to this metamorphosis if a) you know exactly what you want, or b) you don't have the faintest idea of what you want.

Last minute brides who march into the dress shop with their hearts set on one—and only one—particular gown are just asking for a huge disappointment. The picture of the perfect dress they tore out of a bridal magazine may be from the next season's collection (remember, bridal magazines cater to the year-ahead-of-time bride) and may not even be available for months. On the other hand, brides who are completely clueless can wander aimlessly from shop to shop and end up confused and stressed out because they're overwhelmed by the choices and running out of time.

Even though you're on a tight deadline, before you look up the address for a single bridal shop, spend some time thinking about the type of the dress you want and the type of wedding you're planning. What styles generally look good on you, flatter your figure, and make you feel good about yourself? Does your religion have any guidelines or requirements (such as no sleeveless or low-cut gowns) you need to adhere to? Do you want white, ivory, or some other color? What type of weather can you expect at the time of year when you'll be getting married? Will the wedding be formal, casual, or something in-between? How much money do you want to spend?

Look through current bridal magazines or browse some of the Internet wedding sites (listed in Appendix B) to get an idea of what's out there and maybe even narrow down the basic styles you'd like to try on once you go shopping. By thinking through all of these issues and doing your homework before you hit the stores, you'll increase your odds of enjoying your dress-buying experience—or at least diminish the amount of stress it'll cause.

So, where do you go to find a wedding dress in a hurry? Most bridal shops sell at least some wedding gowns off the rack, although the selection of styles and sizes may be limited. Make sure you allow enough time for alterations. If you have a couple of months before your wedding, you may be able to order a dress from a bridal shop catalog. Depending on the time of year, however, some of the styles may not be available on short notice.

When searching for the perfect wedding gown, you might want to consider off-white, ivory, or white bridesmaids' dresses. Dresses in this section of the bridal shop, while still elegant, tend to be less fussy than formal wedding gowns, and prices for bridesmaids' dresses are also usually lower.

Comparison-shop at several bridal stores as you look for your dress. If you find a dress you like at one store, you may be able to get the salesperson to lower the price or throw in free alterations if you know how much comparable dresses are selling for at other stores.

If you're on a tight budget or just hate the idea of paying more for a dress than for a good used car, check consignment and secondhand shops and the classifieds in your local newspaper. Sometimes you'll run across gowns that the bride-to-be never even wore.

Several wedding Web sites listed in Appendix B include links for readers who want to sell their wedding gowns to other readers. Although they're called classified ads, these are vastly different from the ones in your local newspaper. With a local ad for a wedding dress, you can go and look at the dress, check out its quality and condition, and even try it on. You know right away, without any money ever changing hands, if the dress will work for you and is worth the money. With a dress advertised through an Internet classified ad, it's not that easy. As they're described online, the gowns are all gorgeous, in excellent condition, and are a tremendous bargain. That sounds good, but think a minute before you dash off an e-mail to the seller: You can't try the dress on before you buy it and you can't return it if you don't like it or if it turns out to be completely different from the way the ad describes it. Sure, the overwhelming majority of ads on these sites are probably authentic and submitted by responsible, warm, and loving people who just want to make the world a better place, but do you really want to take the chance that you'll find the one that's not—especially when you have so little time for mistakes? Maybe if you're buying a set of potholders you could risk shopping sight-unseen, but think twice about taking that chance with your wedding dress.

Another wedding-dress option is to hire a seamstress, although you're going to be cutting it close if your wedding is less than a couple of months away. Aside from the time it'll take to make the dress, allow two to four weeks to

Last Minute Weddings

order fabric and any other materials (beads, lace, etc.) your seamstress will need. You'll also want to schedule at least two fittings and allow time to have the dress cleaned and pressed well before the big day.

A word about finding a seamstress: Don't just pick one out of the phone book. For something as important as your wedding dress, use only a seamstress you trust completely. Get recommendations from friends, your dry cleaner, or a high-end clothing shop in your area that does alterations. Contact other brides she's sewn for and ask not only about the quality of her work, but also how she is to work with. You may find the most talented seamstress in the continental United States, but if she's got a nasty attitude or can't meet a deadline to save her soul, keep looking.

A seamstress may also be your answer if you borrow a dress from a friend or relative. Chances are it won't be a perfect fit, so you'll need to have it altered. (Be sure to get permission from the person you're borrowing the dress from before you allow the seamstress to take her scissors to it!)

If keeping a wedding dress forever isn't important to you, consider renting one. Many shops will loan gowns out for a fraction of the cost of purchasing one. They carry a wide variety of dresses and sizes and will even make alterations for you. Your veil and slip should be included in the rental fee, and the shop will take care of cleaning the dress when you return it (also included in the fee). For the best selection, go shopping as soon as possible and put down a deposit to reserve your gown. Three months ahead of time isn't too early, but you may still be able to find a dress you like the week of your wedding, especially if you're getting married in an off-peak time of year. To find a shop that offers gown rentals, check your phone book under *Bridal Shops*.

The Photographer/Videographer

You'll probably never wear your wedding dress again, your guests will be hungry a few hours after the food at the reception is cleared away, and your bouquet will wilt while you're on your honeymoon. All that will remain as a reminder of your special day (aside from your new mate, of course) are your wedding photos and videotapes. Because they're so important, this is one area where you shouldn't cut corners. That's not to say you have to seek out the most expensive photographer or videographer in town or call the whole thing off if she's unavailable. (Of course the world is full of trained, professional *male* photographers who are excellent at what they do. In this section, however, we will use the pronoun "she" simply for ease of reading and hope not to insult any male photographers with this choice.) But don't put your photos and memories in the hands of someone who'll give you a good deal because she's thinking about making a career change from accounting to photography/videotaping and wants to use your wedding as a test.

Photographer

Good photographers book up very quickly, especially during the peak wedding months, so start looking as soon as possible. Most won't charge extra for a last-minute booking, but finding one who is available on short notice can be tricky. February (except for Valentine's Day) and March are typically slow months, but even if you're getting married during the peak wedding season, you'll increase your chances of finding a good photographer on short notice if your wedding is on a day other than Saturday.

Begin your search for a photographer by getting recommendations from friends, relatives, co-workers—anyone you know who's gotten married recently. Make sure any

Last Minute Weddings

photographers you consider are experienced in *wedding photography.* It takes skill, diplomacy, and patience to keep an excited wedding party rounded up, move flower girls and grandparents on and off the stage for photos, make the ring bearer stand still long enough to snap a shot, and keep the cameras loaded with film—all in less than 45 minutes so wedding guests won't get restless waiting for the newlyweds to arrive at the reception. A person may be a terrific nature photographer, but the skills required to shoot pictures of a flock of migrating geese are considerably different from those needed to photograph a herd of giddy family members and bridesmaids. You'll be much happier with both the experience of being photographed and the final product when the photos are taken by someone who knows what she is doing.

When you meet with a prospective photographer, look through her sample albums to see if you like her style. Check out the quality of both the formal posed photos and the candid action shots to see if she can handle both types equally well. If you're dealing with a large studio with several photographers on staff, ask who will take your photos and look at that person's work. (Be sure your contract names that photographer specifically.) Ask for references and call them. Discuss any special needs or requests you have and hammer out all of the particulars before you sign a contract. You'll want to ask the following.

Is the photographer flexible and willing to take pictures in the sequence you want? For example, if you don't want to see your groom on your wedding day until you walk down the aisle, is she willing to take photos of you separately before the ceremony and save the couple shots for afterwards?

Will she shoot more than just her standard poses? Be sure to give her a detailed list—well before the wedding—

of any special photos you'd like taken (for example, your new spouse dancing with your grandmother at the reception) or any particular people you'd like photographed. If you want candids as well as posed photos, let her know that as well.

Has she ever photographed a wedding in the location where yours will be held? Some religious facilities have specific guidelines for when and where a flash may be used and allow photographers to take pictures during the ceremony only from a designated spot. Provide all the information she'll need ahead of time so there won't be any surprises. She may even want to check the place out in person so she'll know what to expect on your wedding day.

How does she charge for her services? Some photographers charge by the hour, some by the roll, some per print, and some offer package deals. Try to arrange at least partial payment when the proofs or the finished prints are delivered so you'll have some leverage if she doesn't come through with everything she promised. Make sure the terms are spelled out in your contract.

What happens if the photographer has an accident or sudden illness right before the wedding? Large studios can usually send another photographer on the staff in case of an emergency, and independent photographers may be able to call in a colleague from another studio. Find out exactly what the contingency plan is.

How long will it take to receive the proofs? The prints?

How long will she keep the negatives on file? This is important to know if you're planning or even that thinking you might order reprints in the future.

Finally, judge the photographer not only by the quality of photos she takes, but also by her personality and mannerisms. You may find an expert photographer with tons of experience and all the right credentials, but if she treats you like an idiot or is rude and annoying, think seriously about looking elsewhere. Your photographer will interact directly with you, your wedding party, and your guests— don't let one of the happiest days of your life be spoiled by a grumpy photographer.

A word of warning: If your wedding is during a peak month and you've waited until the *very* last minute to plan it, there's a possibility that you won't be able to find a professional wedding photographer who's available to take pictures. You do have another alternative, but look into it only when you've exhausted all other options. Call the art department at your local junior college, college, or university and speak with a photography instructor. If luck is with you, he or she may be able to recommend a standout student or acquaintance who would be willing to take pictures for you. Camera shops in town may also be able to put you in touch with a talented amateur photographer. If you go this route, designate a friend or relative—preferably one with strong organizational and people skills—to work with your photographer. Give her a list of photos you want taken and put her in charge of assembling those who'll be photographed and keeping the photo shoot moving. All the photographer will have to do is tell people where to stand and then shoot the pictures. Although this is not an ideal solution, it's better than taking your Uncle Howard up on his offer to wander around during the ceremony with his Instamatic.

Videographer

Twenty years ago, couples preserved the sounds of their wedding on audiotape. Today, they can capture the sights as well as the sounds on video and even add a little drama and nostalgia to the whole production.

Videographers—professionals, not just a friend with a camcorder—are becoming increasingly common at weddings. Good ones can turn your wedding into a story by integrating music, photos of you and your beloved as you were growing up and dating, and shots of prewedding events and the reception with the footage of your ceremony. You can ask them to work with your vision of how your story should be told or you can leave the creativity up to them.

To find a good videographer, get recommendations from friends or check the yellow pages. You'll want to ask prospective videographers many of the questions you asked the photographers you interviewed, but there are some things specific to making videos you should investigate.

First, make sure the videographers you interview have experience shooting weddings. View some of the wedding videos they've made and check for image and sound quality as well as the style in which they were put together. Note the differences between videos using one camera and those using two so you can decide which you prefer. Ask about turnaround time (it should be one week or less) and if they make custom covers for the videos. Finally, find out if they keep a master copy (and if so, for how long) in case your copies are lost, damaged, or destroyed.

Along with the Big Four, the must-haves are the core around which all the other aspects of your wedding will revolve. Once you have an officiant, the marriage license, your wedding dress, and a photographer, you can breathe a sigh of relief. No matter what happens with all the other arrangements, you have in your pocket all you really need to get married (assuming the groom will be there as well!).

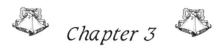

Chapter 3

Ceremony Niceties

The ceremony niceties are your wedding colors, the attire for the wedding party, invitations, flowers, decorations, music, the rehearsal dinner, and a few extra frills. These are the things that make your wedding, well, nice. Your vows will still be valid whether or not your bridesmaids wear matching outfits or your guests have bubbles to blow as you leave the church. But the ceremony niceties allow your personality, taste, and sense of style to shine through. They make your wedding uniquely yours.

Your Wedding Colors

Selecting the colors for your wedding is like opening one of those megaboxes of crayons and deciding which ones you'll use on the prettiest picture in your new coloring book. There are so many to choose from, but you want the ones you pick to be perfect. Although your likes and dislikes play an important part in coloring the perfect picture, there are a few other factors to think about as well.

Color sets a mood, so consider how people perceive different shades. For example, bright yellow is warm and sunny and creates a cheerful, light atmosphere. On the other hand, hunter green is dramatic and sophisticated and carries an air of formality. Think about the mood you want to create and choose colors that evoke those feelings.

Consider the time of year you're getting married and what colors will be most readily available in everything from bridesmaids' dresses and flowers to ribbons and candles. Anything you have to special order will take extra time—time you may not have—and cost more than seasonal items. For example, you can find light lavender dresses and brightly-colored tulips in a million places in April, but you'd be hard pressed to find any at all in November. Even if you could find them, springtime colors would look out of place in the fall.

Think about your wedding party as well when choosing colors. If your maid of honor is a flaming redhead, she probably won't appreciate being dressed head to toe in cotton-candy pink. And if you're planning to incorporate your colors into the groomsmen's clothing with anything more than a matching boutonniere—maybe a vest or a cummerbund—pick a color they won't pitch a fit over. You have enough to deal with in planning your wedding, you don't need a hostile wedding party to complicate things.

Dressing the Women in Your Wedding

Put a group of women in a room, show them a dress you think is absolutely stunning, and tell them they're going to wear it—in public!—and you're likely to get a wide range of responses. If your wedding party is like most, the bridesmaids are of various shapes, sizes, and ages, and probably don't all share your taste in clothing. Choosing a single style that will both satisfy your vision of your wedding and keep your bridesmaids from wanting to jump off the nearest cliff can be a daunting task. But hundreds of thousands of brides figure out a solution to this dilemma every year, so can you, just faster.

Last Minute Weddings

Before you head to the bridal shop to pick out bridesmaids' dresses, consider your attendants' financial situations. Standing up for someone at a wedding can be very expensive. If your attendants are starving college students or are struggling to make ends meet, it's a bad idea to put them in a financial stranglehold by asking them to spend hundreds of dollars on a dress they may never wear again. Keep the cost of their clothing to a level that's manageable for them or pay for their outfits yourself.

Look through some bridal magazines to get an idea of a style that will match your wedding plans. Your attendants' outfits should complement your dress in both style and degree of formality. For example, if you've chosen a simple, uncluttered tea-length dress for your afternoon wedding, don't put your bridesmaids in velvet floor-length gowns with intricate beadwork and rows of lace. Your attendants should look like they belong in your wedding, not the one at the church next door.

Bridal shops are the most obvious place to begin your search for your bridesmaids' dresses. As with bridal gowns, most shops sell some attendants' dresses off the rack, but the selection of styles and sizes will be limited. Unless your wedding party is very small, the store will probably not have enough of the same dress to outfit all of your attendants. If you find one you like, though, ask how long it will take to order it for all your attendants. Most dresses take about three months to arrive, but some manufacturers can ship them more quickly.

A ready supply of both formal and informal dresses is often available at most higher-end department stores. The styles are usually more trendy and don't have that "bridesmaidy" look that bridal shop dresses often do, so your attendants may get more than one wearing out of their outfits. Department stores also tend to stock greater quantities and more sizes than bridal shops. If you find a style you like but you can't find some of the sizes you need, the salesperson might be able to locate them for you at one of the store's other branches. This is a much faster route for the last minute wedding.

Department store catalogs are another option. Many catalogs carry bridesmaids' and flower girls' dresses, and delivery time is much shorter than it is for bridal shops. Most of the dresses come in a wide range of colors and sizes, and you can return them if you find you don't like them. (See Appendix A for a listing of some of the national stores that offer these dresses through a catalog.)

Tip: If you're extremely short on time, you can dress your bridesmaids in long black skirts and white blouses and have them carry long-stemmed roses. Beautiful. Elegant. Fast.

Flower girl

Many flower girls wear frilly white dresses that mimic the bride's, or they wear outfits that match the bridesmaids' dresses. If you have enough time to special-order your bridesmaids' dresses, you should have time to order the flower girl's dress as well. But if you're buying off the rack, this can be tough to pull off with a last minute wedding. The odds are against finding a miniature version of a bridal or bridesmaid's dress in stock and available in your flower girl's size. But don't despair. Because your flower girl probably won't walk beside anyone but the ring bearer, you can certainly put her in something that complements the bridesmaids' dresses but isn't a carbon copy. Most children's shops and higher-end department stores carry fancy little girls' dresses in a variety of colors, styles, and sizes—chances are good that you'll find an outfit that will work for your flower girl.

Dressing the Men in Your Wedding

Compared to dressing the women in your wedding party, finding outfits for the men to wear is a snap. The most common wedding apparel for the groom, groomsmen, ushers, and ring bearer is a tuxedo, with black being the leading color. You can incorporate your color scheme into their clothing with a matching vest, cummerbund, or boutonniere. Because few men and even fewer boys own tuxedos, most rent them from a bridal or formal wear shop. If they don't have appropriate shoes to wear with the tux, they can rent those as well.

After you and your fiancé pick out the style you like, have the men go to the shop at least a month before the wedding (two to three months if you're getting married in a peak month) to be fitted for and reserve their tuxedos. If a groomsman is an out-of-towner, ask him to get measured and sized for a tuxedo at a formal wear shop in his local area and send you the measurements so you can reserve a tux for him.

While a tux is most common, there are many alternatives. It's hard to find anything more formal than military men standing shoulder to shoulder in dress uniforms (although this only works if your groom is in the military). For a less formal wedding, the men can wear suits with ties in the wedding colors or even matching slacks and sweaters. And jeans paired with tuxedo jackets is a great look for weddings with a western flair.

The key to making the groomsmen show up wearing outfits that match the style of your wedding is all in the timing. It's not easy to get a group of guys to cooperate about getting measured for clothing but you don't have time to fool around. Make it a priority to nag each one of them incessantly until they all order their clothing.

Invitations

The first step in choosing your wedding invitations is to make up a guest list. You may be so deliriously happy about your upcoming nuptials that you want to invite everyone in a 50-mile radius, but unless you live in a very sparsely populated area, you'll need to be a bit more selective. There are several factors to consider before you start writing down names.

First, how many people can your wedding and reception facility accommodate? Don't invite more guests than will fit comfortably for the activities you're planning. For example, your reception facility may accommodate 200 people if you throw a cake-and-punch celebration where everyone stands around and mingles for a couple of hours. But it may only be able to handle half that number if you are going to seat everyone at tables and serve a full meal.

Second, keep your budget in mind. The more guests you invite, the more you'll spend, and not just on invitations. As your guest list grows, the cost for things like food and drinks at the reception, wedding favors, and even postage for the invitations will increase as well. If you have a large circle of family and friends and it's important to invite them all, you can stay within your budget by cutting back in other areas. You might, for example, skip the wedding favors and programs or choose flowers that are in season instead of ones you'll have to special order.

With an approximate number agreed upon, sit down with your fiancé and make a list of the people you want to witness your nuptials. The people on this list should be your friends and loved ones, not the client you want to impress or the brother of the friend of your college roommate who you went out with once and whose feelings might be hurt if he's not invited. Get your parents' (and your fiancé's parents') input on the list—more than likely, they'll remember to include Aunt Diane and Uncle Bob even if you didn't. They may also have some names they'd like to add to the list.

This is where it could get dicey. If the number of people on your list is about the same as your target number of invitees, start shopping for invitations. But if you have a lot more people than you do places to put them, you'll either have to whittle down the list or figure out a way to include everyone. Try to consider the feelings of everyone involved—your future spouse, both sets of parents, and you—as you work together to bring the list to a more manageable size.

Traditional invitations

Your guests will get their first peek at your wedding through the invitation. It sets the tone, gives a glimpse of your personality, and even helps recipients decide how to dress for the occasion. Because it can make such a strong statement, take your time as you make your choice (but not too much time!). Think about the style of your wedding and make the invitations match—a gilded, formal invitation, for instance, may not be the best choice for a blue-jean wedding and barbecue reception.

Bridal, stationery, and party supply shops carry books with hundreds of invitations to choose from. They run the gamut from cute and casual to formal and fancy, and most have coordinating response cards, thank you notes, wedding programs, and envelopes. Costs vary as much as designs, so you should be able to find one to fit both your taste and your budget. Before you fall in love with any invitation, though, ask the salesperson about turnaround times for specific stationers. Some will have your order returned within a week or two while others typically take a month or more to deliver. Because you should mail your invitations about six weeks before your wedding, and you'll need at least a week to get them all addressed and stamped, consider whether you have time to wait a month for your order to come in. If you don't, stay away from the slower printers.

An option for purchasing wedding invitations if you're on an extremely tight schedule is to have them custom designed by a local print shop. This can be an expensive proposition, but most printers can rush an order through if you're willing to pay for it.

Another alternative is to order your wedding invitations through the mail. (See Appendix B for a list of mail-order invitation companies.) Turnaround is as fast as 24 to 48 hours, and reputable companies offer money-back guarantees. Many of the products they sell are identical to the ones you'll find at bridal shops and stationery stores, but the prices tend to be lower. Catalogs feature full-color photographs of the invitations and coordinating pieces (response cards, programs, envelopes, etc.), and you can request samples of any invitations you're interested in (which you *definitely* want to do before ordering). If you don't know what to say in your invitation, the catalogs provide samples of both traditional inscriptions and inscriptions that reflect a variety of circumstances and family structures. Some companies even have staff wedding consultants you can call toll free to ask for advice. And as added plus: Most of these catalogs also carry wedding accessories, such as unity candles, cake servers and toppers, garters, toasting goblets, guest books, and decorations, so you can save time shopping for those items too.

Traditionally, wedding invitations are engraved. In recent years, however, a much more economical printing method—thermography—has become very popular. Thermography produces raised lettering that's virtually identical to engraving. The difference in appearance between the two styles is visible only on the back—engraved invitations have indentations from the engraving plate; the backs of thermography-printed invitations are smooth. Depending on the number you're ordering, you can pay for most—if not all—of your stamps with the money you'll save by printing instead of engraving your invitations.

Overestimate your needs when you order your invitations so you're sure to have enough and won't waste time reordering. You can bet you'll need to add people to your guest list after you've placed your order for invitations. It's significantly cheaper to buy an extra 25 invitations initially than it is to pay for setting up the press for a new run of 25 invitations later (and on your tight schedule, this could be a disaster!).

While you wait for your invitations to arrive, collect and verify addresses of the people on your guest list and make sure you have the correct spelling of their names. Buy stamps and any special pens you'll need for addressing the envelopes. If you've hired or recruited a calligrapher, let him or her know the approximate delivery date and deadline for getting the invitations out to your guests.

Tip: If there are out-of-towners on your guest list, address and mail their invitations first so they'll have more time to make their travel arrangements. And be sure to put a few invitations aside as keepsakes for yourself.

Alternatives to traditional invitations

Maybe you can't or don't want to spend the time or the money ordering invitations from a stationer or printer. If you're proficient with a PC and have access to a good laser printer, you can create your own in a few hours and for much less than you'd pay for traditional invitations. Some office supply stores, specialty paper shops, and mail-order wedding supply companies carry wedding invitation kits that contain 25 blank invitations (they come in a variety of designs), note cards, envelopes, and even the software you'll need to print your own traditional-looking invitations. The kit costs around $25, and you can buy additional packs of invitations or note cards separately. If you're looking for something far from traditional, you can also find postcards, stationery, and matching envelopes in a huge variety of designs and colors—from vibrant geometrics to soft florals to subtle textures. Office supply stores and specialty paper mail-order houses also sell template software—all you have to do is type your copy into a placeholder, spell-check, and print. (See Appendix B for a list of companies that sell these supplies online and through catalogs.)

If you have an artistic bent, you may be considering handcrafting your own invitations. Craft and art supply stores stock professional-quality materials that you can use to create invitations that will express your feelings and personality better than any store-bought invitation ever could. The problem with combining handcrafted invitations and last minute weddings, however, is time. If you're planning a traditional wedding and you only have two months to pull it all together, spending three weeks making 150 invitations may not be the wisest use of your time.

But if having unique invitations means a lot to you, you can make it happen. Maybe you have a friend or group of friends who are artsy like you. Design your invitation, make a prototype or two, buy all of the materials you'll need, and invite your friends over for an invitation-making all-nighter. Be sure to design your invitations so they'll fit into envelopes you can purchase or you'll have to have an envelope-making all-nighter as well.

Flowers and Decorations

The more popular florists tend to book quickly during the peak wedding season, so you have the best chance of finding a good florist on short notice if your wedding falls in an off-peak month or on a day other than Saturday. But whenever it is, with a little determination you'll certainly be able to find a florist who is available on short notice. Check with smaller shops and those that haven't been in business long enough to have a widespread reputation. Small, startup companies will often bend over backwards for you and give you the kind of personalized service you won't get from the big guys anyway. To make sure the florist can handle the job, though, ask for references from couples he or she has done weddings for in the past.

You can also look into florists associated with grocery and department stores. Many can arrange and deliver all of the flowers you'll need and in a much shorter amount of time. They usually charge significantly less than a specialty florist and may offer a discount if you buy your wedding cake from the store's bakery. Before you make an appointment to meet with the florist, look through her sample books and make sure she has experience with wedding arrangements.

If you prefer dried or silk flowers, check with craft and wedding supply stores—they usually have people on staff or can recommend someone who can handle your wedding flowers. An added bonus with silk or dried flowers: They can be made up and delivered weeks before your wedding so you'll know exactly what they look like ahead of time. If there are any problems, you've got time to fix them.

Flowers and decorations are one area where you can easily cut corners if you're short on time, money, or both. Walking down the aisle carrying a single rose with its stem wrapped in ribbon can be just as elegant as hauling a massive bouquet filled with exotic tropical flowers. Decorate candelabras in greenery and dried instead of fresh flowers. Use candles and tiny white Christmas lights to create atmosphere, and attach bows instead of floral arrangements to the ends of pews. Avoid the expense of special ordering uncommon flowers by buying those that are in season and readily available. Rent large plants and potted trees from a nursery (inexpensive, and they'll deliver and pick them up) rather than buying elaborate floral arrangements.

Make your wedding decorations do double duty by delegating someone to take flowers and any other easily-transportable decorations from your wedding location to your reception site. Have your bridesmaids place their bouquets on the serving tables and the guest book table at the reception. For more ideas on decorating with (and without) flowers, go to one of the many wedding chat rooms on the Internet, especially those with an emphasis on wedding crafts and decorations (see the list in Appendix B), or visit your local craft store.

Music for the Ceremony

Your first step in choosing the music for your wedding ceremony is to find out what your options are. What instruments (organ, piano, keyboard) are available at your wedding site? Do you have to provide the musicians or are their services part of the cost of using the facility? What can the musicians play and how competent are they?

Many religious facilities have guidelines about the type of music a couple can play at their wedding. Some clergy allow only religious songs, others permit only live—not recorded—music, and some allow a mix of religious and secular, but they want to approve the selections. Check the policies with the staff before you decide on your music so you won't have to scrap your plans and start over (a real waste of time).

If you plan to use recorded music, make sure the wedding site has a top-notch sound system and you have high-quality recordings (with backup recordings of each song in case something happens to the original). Have a competent professional at the controls and be sure he or she attends the rehearsal so you can run through the ceremony with the music. Give this person a printed sequence of events for the ceremony so he or she knows exactly what songs to play and when.

Choose music that complements the style of your wedding and is in keeping with the atmosphere you want to create. If you don't know where to start, don't waste too much time hemming and hawing. Go right to the professionals. Someone on the staff at the wedding site should be able to assist you in picking out your music (they do this all the time). And you can also get ideas from the Internet Web site www.ultimatewedding.com. It lists the most popular wedding songs and links you to a site where you can purchase the music.

Rehearsal and Rehearsal Dinner

Typically, the rehearsal and rehearsal dinner are held the night before the wedding. Ideally, you'll rehearse at the facility where your wedding will be held. But with the last minute arrangement, you may not be able to reserve the site for both the rehearsal and the wedding. Don't let this worry you. As long as everyone involved in the ceremony is available, you can rehearse just about anywhere.

By the time you've gotten this far, you and your fiancé will have decided on what you want in your ceremony and discussed the sequence of events with your officiant. Because the officiant has performed many weddings and knows the most efficient and effective way to run a rehearsal, he or she will take the lead. You'll probably have to go through the ceremony a couple of times to work out the bugs and to make sure your musicians and/or sound people have their timing down.

After the rehearsal, it's traditional to have a rehearsal dinner, usually hosted by the groom's family at a restaurant or hotel banquet room. Arrangements for the dinner should be made a month or two before the wedding. But if you're working on a tight schedule, remember that many restaurants will accept last minute reservations. If you go to a restaurant, ask if your party can order a la carte or if you need to choose a limited menu and pay a fixed price per person.

When setting your rehearsal date, keep in mind that some popular restaurants may not accept reservations for groups or parties for Friday or Saturday nights. Not to worry—there's no rule that says you have to rehearse your wedding on the night immediately before the wedding, or in the evening, or that your rehearsal dinner even has to be a dinner. Hold your rehearsal in the morning and have a rehearsal breakfast, brunch, or luncheon. Not only is the restaurant likely to be less crowded, but the cost may be lower as well. Or give everyone a chance to relax before the big day by catering a rehearsal picnic or barbecue.

Your rehearsal dinner should be a time for you to have fun with the people who are closest to you. It's also a great opportunity for you to give a gift of appreciation to all of your attendants and the people who are helping you pull your wedding together (see Chapter 5).

The Frills

For the most part, everything in this section is optional or can be taken care of very quickly. If you run short on time or if the things discussed here just aren't a priority for you, skip them.

Programs

Wedding programs are becoming more and more popular. They list the ceremony's sequence of events, recognize the members of the wedding party, and thank guests for sharing the couple's special day. The couple can also honor a relative who has recently passed away or send some other message to guests.

You can often find programs that match your wedding invitations. But don't order them until you've finalized the ceremony, your wedding party, and the music.

You can also print your own programs. Appendix B lists specialty paper companies that carry blank cards and brochures in a huge variety of styles and colors (see *Invitations* in this chapter for more information). You can order and print them quickly—a great advantage when you're in a hurry or if there are any last minute changes.

Rice, birdseed, bubbles, and more

Rice used to be the projectile of choice to hurl at newlyweds as they left the wedding, but now very few wedding facilities permit it because of its damaging effect on birds who eat it. Birdseed succeeded rice, but it has fallen into disfavor as well—too many people have found themselves on the ground after slipping on the little pellets.

Bubbles packaged in tiny bottles decorated specifically for weddings are gaining in popularity and are available through bridal shops, craft, party, and wedding supply stores, and mail-order wedding catalogs. These places also carry sparkly confetti shaped like hearts and bells, special heart-shaped wedding rice, and little bells guests can jingle as you leave the church or reception hall. Another idea is flower petals—leave them loose in baskets so guests can grab a handful on their way out the door or tie them into little net bags secured with colorful ribbons.

Check with your wedding facility about the policy on farewell items before you buy anything. Some won't allow bubbles or real flower petals because they can leave stains on carpets (bubbles can also stain your dress and sting if they get in your eyes) or confetti because it's not biodegradable and it's hard to clean up.

The list of niceties is long, but the results are worth it. Your wedding colors, the attire for the wedding party, the invitations, flowers, decorations, music, rehearsal, and all the other frills combine in the end (even at the last minute) to create the kind of wedding you've always dreamed of.

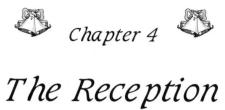

Chapter 4

The Reception

Most couples follow a pretty basic pattern when it comes to the wedding ceremony—get a bunch of bridesmaids and groomsmen, march down the aisle, exchange vows, kiss, march back up the aisle. The end.

When it comes to the reception, though, the rule book goes out the window. You can plan a simple gathering with cake, punch, and soft music playing in the background. Make it a little more involved with an hors d'oeuvres buffet and a DJ. Or go all out with a sit-down dinner and a 14-piece orchestra. It's your party, so it's your call.

Food and Drinks

Your budget will play a major role in how elaborate or simple a reception you have. For a cake-and-punch reception, your expenses are minimal—you can easily serve 100 people for a few hundred dollars. You can count on spending at least $12 to $15 per person for a simple catered buffet without alcoholic beverages. When you move up to a catered sit-down meal with an open bar, you're looking at $50 to $75 per person.

Check with a representative from your reception facility about the policies on food. Some require that you use in-house catering services for any food or beverages you serve (except for wedding cake—most allow you to bring that in). Some recommend a particular caterer and will give you a discount on your room rental fee if you use that service, and others allow you to use any caterer you want or to bring the food in yourself.

The summer months are the most difficult time to find a caterer on short notice. If you're planning your wedding for the summer, start looking no less than two months before the wedding. At other times of the year, you can usually find one available with as little as two weeks' notice.

To find a caterer, get referrals from friends, check the yellow pages, or ask someone from your reception facility to recommend a company that has catered events at that location before.

When you meet with prospective caterers, ask lots of questions. Discuss your budget, the number of guests you expect, the type of food you'd like to serve, and how you want to serve it (buffet or sit-down). Look through any photo albums they may have of weddings and other events they've catered and ask for references. Ask to sample their food and arrange to attend (or at least take a peek at) an event they'll cater in the future in which they'll serve food similar to what you want. Also find out what their cancellation policy is, what recourse you have if you're not satisfied with their service, how much of a deposit you're required to put down, and when the balance is due.

In your contract, specify the menu, services the caterer will perform (set up, wait tables, tend bar, stock tables, clean up, etc.), supplies they'll provide (dishes, table linens, silverware, etc.), the cost, location, date, and time of your reception.

If you can't find a caterer on short notice, don't panic—there are other avenues to explore. Call local colleges and universities that have culinary arts departments—some of the students training to be chefs may jump at the chance to gain some real-world experience catering an event. Contact your local cooking club to see if the group or some members of the group would be interested in helping you out and raising some money either for themselves or the club.

Many brides opt to skip the caterer and do the cooking themselves. If you decide on this option, keep one thing in mind—good food doesn't have to be elaborate food. Don't use complicated recipes that require split-second timing, optimum atmospheric conditions, and constant babysitting. You'll have enough to do (and so will your mom and anyone else you recruit to help) without having to worry about your crepes flopping or your soufflés falling.

If you decide to cook your own food, take shortcuts wherever you can—buy baby carrots instead of peeling, trimming, and slicing whole carrots, for example—and do as much ahead of time as possible. Those huge warehouse stores where you can buy food in bulk often carry prepared dishes, such as miniquiches and frozen Swedish meatballs that are of excellent quality and are a snap to make. Look through cookbooks and magazines for ideas but be sure to make a practice batch or two of any recipe you're considering using.

When you're planning your home-cooked menu, decide if you need to rent or buy any special dishes or equipment, such as chafing dishes or ice containers, to keep hot foods hot and cold foods cold. Recruit a couple of friends to keep an eye on the food during the reception and to keep all of the dishes replenished and at the proper temperature.

If you don't want to spend the week before your wedding in the kitchen and you can't find an available caterer, it's still not time to scream. You can pull a buffet together using resources you may not have considered before. Most grocery stores can prepare nice fruit, vegetable, or meat and cheese trays with just a day or two's notice. You can either give them your own trays or platters or they'll use their own disposable plastic trays with lids. Grocery store deli departments carry cheese balls and prepared salads, while their bakeries make many types of fresh breads and rolls. You can also order a variety of three-foot hoagie or submarine sandwiches from a good sandwich shop, cut them into individual portions, and arrange them on silver trays. If your favorite restaurant makes a killer appetizer, see if you can order a large quantity and have it delivered to your reception location during your wedding (or before, if it's something that will keep). For sweets, check out the selection at bakeries and specialty candy shops in town.

If you go this route, you'll need to fill in some of the holes a caterer would have taken care of—mustard and mayonnaise for the meat/cheese/breads, toothpicks for the fruit, dip for the vegetable tray, serving dishes to keep foods at their proper temperature, etc. Also have a couple of people in charge of keeping the table well stocked and clearing away dirty dishes.

If you plan to serve alcohol, including champagne for toasting, check the local laws and regulations about dispensing liquor. They vary widely from state to state, but your caterer or someone from your reception facility should be able to advise you on any requirements you'll need to meet. (A word of warning: In some states, a host who serves alcohol at a party can be held liable if an intoxicated guest leaves the party and is involved in an accident.)

If you don't use a caterer (and sometimes even if you do), you'll have to provide the dishes, utensils, glassware, and table linens for your reception. Check first with a representative from your reception facility—he or she may have some or all of what you need. If not, you can either rent or buy it.

Rental service and party supply stores carry a wide range of reception supplies from glassware and dishes to tables and tents. Because most of these stores stock the items in a number of colors and styles, you should go to the stores and browse through their displays instead of ordering sight-unseen on the phone. If your wedding is at an off-peak time of year, you may be able to reserve items as late as the week before. During the summer months, four to six weeks ahead of time should be sufficient.

For a more informal reception, you might consider using paper plates and plastic cups and utensils. Wedding and party supply stores carry paper and plastic products in a huge variety of colors and designs. They also carry coordinating plastic tablecloths and table skirts in several shapes and sizes. If you use disposable dishes, be sure to have plenty of trash cans available so trash doesn't pile up.

A final word on the subject of the food you serve at your reception: You and your new spouse will probably be so busy visiting with guests that, unless you have a formal sit-down meal, you won't have a chance to eat much, if anything. Arrange for someone to prepare a couple of take-out boxes of food for you so you won't have to stop at McDonald's when you leave the reception.

The Wedding Cake

The crowning glory of your reception food is your wedding cake. Traditional wedding cakes are round and tiered, but many bakers offer unique styles and designs. The groom's cake has also become popular in recent years—this can be a sheet or round tier cake and come in any size, shape, color, or flavor. The cake's design usually reflects some interest or hobby the groom has and may have his name on it somewhere. To find the baker who is right for you, look through different bakeries' photo albums until you find one with just the right style and creativity.

Most bakers prefer to have your order about two months ahead of time, especially during peak months, but some can make a cake with just a few weeks' or even days' notice. If you run into trouble because of your tight schedule, try the bakery at your local grocery store. The lead time there is usually much shorter than at a specialty baker's (many routinely bake wedding and groom's cakes with a week or two's notice) and their prices are considerably less. An added plus: Store bakers can work with the store florist if you want fresh flowers on the cake.

Be prepared with a list of questions when you meet with a prospective baker. Ask about the flavors and varieties (of both cake and frosting). Sample any of the cakes you're interested in and be sure to choose varieties that slice easily and won't crumble. If you plan to incorporate your wedding colors in the wedding cake, provide a swatch of the bridesmaids' fabric or a piece of the ribbon you'll use in decorations or floral arrangements. Find out the baker's policy on cake plates, trays, and tiers—some require a deposit, others don't. The bakery may have decorative cake toppers for sale or rent, but you can also check wedding supply stores or mail-order catalogs if the bakery doesn't have a topper you like. Ask if you will get a box for saving the top tier of the wedding cake. When discussing costs, ask if the price quote includes delivery and set up of the cakes (some bakeries charge extra).

Music and Dancing

If you intend to dance all night, make sure you've got the music to do it with. Whether you have live or recorded music depends on your tastes and your budget. But keep

Last Minute Weddings

in mind that generally speaking, a live band will cost significantly (as much as two times) more than a DJ and may be more difficult to book at short notice.

Word-of-mouth is a good way to find a band that plays the kind of music you like, but you may also find musicians through a local contact service (look under *Musicians* or *Entertainers* in the yellow pages). It's impossible to say definitively how far in advance you should look for a band because every city and town is different, but obviously, the earlier you look, the better your chances will be of finding a good one that's available on your date.

When making your selection, don't judge a band by a video or audiotape they may give you. Tapes can be doctored to make groups look and sound better than they actually are. Listen to them in person. Before you commit to hiring a band, arrange to attend an event they will be playing so you can see how they interact with the crowd and how the crowd reacts to them. Listen to the quality of their instruments and sound system, and notice if they play a wide repertoire of songs. This will take up a few nights of your free time, but it's worth it.

You may not want an entire band, just a small ensemble or a single violinist or classical guitarist. If you can't find anyone through a contact service, get in touch with the chairperson of the music department at your local university and ask if he or she can recommend a student (or even an instructor) who would be willing and able to play for your wedding and/or reception. Music and instrument stores may also have a list of freelance musicians.

A DJ may be easier to find on short notice than a band, especially if your wedding is during the peak wedding months. DJs have some advantages over live musicians. They usually cost a lot less and can play a greater range of songs. They don't need to take breaks every hour, and they don't "interpret" songs—the way you hear them on the radio is the way you'll hear them from a DJ.

DJs are plentiful, but good DJs are getting hard to come by. Start by asking friends for recommendations and checking the yellow pages under *Disc Jockeys*. As with a live band, watch prospective DJs at work so you can judge their actual performance. Check out their equipment to see if it sounds good and looks professional. See if you like their stage personality—a person who appears normal when you sign the contract can turn into a raving lunatic once he or she gets a hold of a microphone.

Once you find a DJ with a style you like, check out the details. Describe the type of music you and your guests are likely to enjoy and the types you don't want to hear at your wedding. If there are specific songs you want (or absolutely don't want) played, be sure to say so right up front.

Whether you hire a band or a DJ, work out a reception schedule—when things like the bouquet toss, the cake cutting, the toasts, and any announcements you want made should take place. Choose the songs you want played for the special dances (such as your first dance with your new spouse, your groom's dance with his mother, and your dance with your father) before the reception and include these on the schedule as well. Let your DJ or band leader know how active a role you want him or her to take, urging people to get out on the floor when things slow down or just playing songs and taking requests. And make sure your DJ or musicians know how formal or informal your reception will be so they can dress accordingly.

Flowers and Decorations

If flowers and decorations that complement your wedding style and colors are included in the rental of your reception site, you can cross "decorating" off your to-do list.

Last Minute Weddings

But you probably have caught on by now that when you do things last minute, you often have to do them yourself. If that's the case, it takes only a bit of quick thinking and imagination to pull this off on a tight schedule.

Start with your centerpieces. For a reception with a sit-down meal or buffet, you'll need one for each table, as well as for the guest book table and the gift table. For a cake-and-punch reception, on the other hand, you'll only need two centerpieces—one each for the guest book and gift tables. If there's room, you can have a couple of your bridesmaids place their bouquets on either side of the wedding cake to bring your colors to that table. If the servers need more space as they cut the cake, the bouquets can be easily moved.

Although floral arrangements are common centerpieces and always look beautiful, you can be more creative and original when you do things yourself. For example, arrange an assortment of votive and pillar candles on a mirror and scatter colored decorative marbles (sometimes called gems or gemstones) around for an elegant centerpiece that won't block your guests' view of each other. (Your reception facility may have votives you can use; ask before you buy any.) Tie balloon bouquets with long ribbons to baskets of candy kisses for centerpieces that float above your guests' heads and decorate the whole room. Or fill a glass pedestal bowl half full of water and float candles, flowers, or even goldfish in it. Tie a bow around the base and sprinkle sparkly confetti on the tablecloth and you've got a simple but unique centerpiece that won't blow your budget. You can use bows, glass balls, pine cones, baskets, even colorful fruits and vegetables as building blocks for eye-catching decorations if you use a little imagination. Whatever you decide, keep your centerpieces fairly compact so your guests will have room for their plates and glasses.

For your serving tables (buffet tables, cake and drink tables, etc.), incorporate your wedding colors with linens or use white tablecloths and festoon tulle around the front and sides. Sprinkle sparkly confetti all around, adding instant color without taking up any space.

You may want or need to decorate more than just the tables. Before you buy anything, ask a representative from your reception facility about decorations he or she can provide. If the site is the location of many weddings, he or she may have things like linens, candelabras, arches, or backdrops that you can use.

You don't have to spend a lot of money to make your reception hall beautiful. For example, you can rent potted trees from a nursery, cover the containers in shiny colored foil, and wrap tiny white lights around the branches. Set them out around the room, use lots of candles, and keep the lights fairly low—absolutely magical. Or hide an ugly ceiling with hundreds of balloons in your wedding colors. Just fill them with helium a few hours before the wedding and let them loose to bump and bob above your guests' heads.

Look for ways to incorporate the season into your decorating. For an autumn wedding, group pumpkins and gourds of various sizes and shapes in front of corn stalks bundled together with ribbons in your wedding colors. For an unusual effect, spray paint the pumpkins and gourds in your wedding colors and highlight with a light dusting of spray glitter (be sure to try this out before the wedding to see if you like the look). Or use hollowed-out pumpkins as vases for fall flowers, such as mums and marigolds.

If your wedding is soon after the December holidays, turn your reception hall into an evergreen forest. Before Christmas, contact tree lot owners and arrange to take the leftovers (and the stands, if possible) after Christmas.

Most will give the trees to you for free, especially if you explain what they're for. Group all of the trees together—even touching—in one area of your reception hall. Wrap some of them with white lights and attach bows in your wedding colors to some of the branches. This makes a lovely backdrop for a receiving line and can cover up an ugly wall or corner.

For spring and summer weddings, set galvanized buckets and watering cans full of daisies or wildflowers around the room. Potted flowering plants in wrapped or painted containers can also bring in your wedding colors—and for considerably less than floral arrangements.

For more ideas on unique decorations, check out some of the wedding craft chat rooms on the Internet (listed in Appendix B) or visit your local craft stores. And remember, don't try to do everything yourself—recruit an artistic, reliable friend to help you.

The Frills

Just like the ceremony frills, the reception frills are things that are nice to have but are by no means mandatory. If you're short on time or money and you decide to skip them, you're probably the only one who'll notice.

Wedding cameras

Wedding cameras have become hot reception extras. These disposable, single-use cameras are available in a variety of wedding designs and can be personalized for an extra few dollars. You place the cameras on tables around the room so your guests can take candid shots during the reception. Be sure to use the table tents that come with the cameras that tactfully explain that guests should take pictures but leave the cameras behind. Otherwise some guests may think the cameras are wedding favors.

You can buy wedding cameras singly or in multipacks at wedding supply stores and through mail-order catalogs and online wedding sites. Comparison shop carefully—the cost of some packs includes film developing.

Mementos

Mementos are the personalized items you provide for your guests to use at your reception—things like napkins, coasters, and swizzle sticks—that are imprinted with your names and wedding date. Wedding supply stores and mail-order companies carry many types and styles of mementos, which are available in a variety of colors. Although they're relatively inexpensive, pick just one or two items you really like—if everything in the room has your name imprinted on it, nothing stands out as special.

When you're in a hurry, mail-order wedding supply companies can be your best bet for ordering mementos. They can deliver your order in as little as 24 to 48 hours. When you order mementos from a store, you're looking at about a two-week wait.

Wedding favors

Wedding favors are similar to mementos in that they're usually imprinted with the couple's names and wedding date, but favors are meant to go home with the guests. They're a small gift or keepsake to thank guests for sharing the couple's day.

Wedding supply stores and mail-order companies carry a huge assortment of wedding favors, such as bookmarks, personalized fortune cookies, candy bags and boxes, and cookie cutters, to name just a few. You can also come up with your own favors—candy kisses in little net bags tied with ribbon, for example.

Last Minute Weddings

If you provide wedding favors, either put them in baskets by the door so your guests can take one as they leave, or set one at each person's place at the tables (if you serve a sit-down meal).

Your reception is a celebration of your love and wedding vows. Don't let planning it make you crazy. Order the food, drinks, cake, music, and any other frills you want, then kick back and get ready to enjoy one great party.

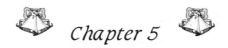

Chapter 5

Things to Think About

There's a lot more to getting married than just planning a wedding and reception. You've got rings to buy, a honeymoon to arrange, and gifts to register for. There are showers and bachelor parties to attend, thank you notes to write, and gifts to buy for your wedding party. And if that's not enough, you've got a marriage to announce after you return home from your honeymoon. Each of these may be on the periphery of your wedding, but they're all important things to think about.

Picking Out the Rings

The most time-consuming part about buying wedding rings is deciding what you want—the rest is a snap. Most jewelry stores have a large selection of wedding sets for the bride and bands for the groom. When you find rings you like, most jewelers can have them sized, engraved, and ready to drive off the lot within one day.

If you'd rather have custom rings, look for a quality jeweler who can design and make them on site—in most cases, your order can be ready in two weeks or less. But if the jeweler has to send custom orders out, it can take up to a month to get your rings.

Prewedding Festivities

Bridal showers, bachelor and bachelorette parties, and prewedding get-togethers are the fun part of getting ready for your wedding.

Bridal showers give friends and family the opportunity to help you and your future mate fill the kitchen cabinets, linen closets, and pantry shelves of your new home. Traditionally, the maid or matron of honor will play hostess, but any friend or group of friends, including your co-workers, can throw a shower in your honor.

The best time for a bridal shower is a couple of weeks or more before the wedding so you're not too busy taking care of the eleventh-hour details to enjoy yourself. If you're really pressed for time, it may be more convenient for you and everyone else involved if your shower is postponed until after you return from your honeymoon.

After finding out about your needs, your hostess may ask guests to bring a particular kind of gift to the shower. For example, she might ask them to bring something for the kitchen, bath, or another room in your home. Or she may throw a lingerie shower to help you fill out your trousseau. She'll want to know what colors you're using to decorate your home, your tastes, and if and where you've registered for china, crystal, linens, and the like so she can let your guests know where to shop.

While showers are traditionally the domain of females, co-ed showers are becoming more and more popular. A couple may hold a shower for you and your fiancé and invite just as many men as women. Gifts given at these co-ed events will include some male-oriented things such as tools and garden or barbecue equipment, giving your fiancé and his friends a chance to put their stamp on the prewedding activities.

Another prewedding activity is the bachelor and/or bachelorette party. Bachelor parties have a pretty bawdy reputation (often well-deserved) but they don't always involve strip joints and wild drinking. Many men view their bachelor party as an opportunity to do one last guy-thing with their buddies before they take the plunge. They may go to a sporting event and out to dinner or take a weekend for a fishing or camping trip together. Traditionally, the best man makes the arrangements for the bachelor party. Talk to this best man about the timing of the bachelor party. Whether it's to be rowdy or sedate, it shouldn't be the night before the wedding. Take it from lots of blurry-eyed grooms—it's just not a good idea.

A bachelorette party is the female version of bachelor party. This, too, can be a somewhat indelicate event if you want it to be. But whether you go to a nightclub or get together for coffee and cheesecake, it's a chance for the bride to have one last night out with the girls. The maid or matron of honor usually spearheads the bachelorette party.

You may also want to make room in your schedule for a get-together with the females in your wedding party. This is especially a good idea if some of them traveled a distance to be in your wedding and you don't see them very often. This can be as simple as taking your bridesmaids, flower girl, mother, future mother-in-law, and any other people you want to include out to breakfast or lunch a day or two before the wedding. The main point of the get-together is for you to spend some relaxed, unstructured time with the women you're closest to.

Attendants' Gifts

In all likelihood, the people in your wedding party are making sacrifices to help you get married. They are buying or renting wedding clothes, giving of their time, and maybe even traveling great distances for you. It's customary to show your thanks for those who take part in your wedding with a special gift. While you don't have to break the bank buying your attendants tokens of your appreciation, you should choose gifts that come from the heart and are a bit more sentimental than the latest Wrestlemania video. Common gifts for bridesmaids are small pieces of jewelry, decorative trinket boxes, or silver picture frames. For men, desk sets, personalized mugs, and engraved money clips are traditional. If you don't know your flower girl and ring bearer well, you may want to ask their mother(s) for gift ideas for them. Others who help with your wedding, such as ushers, cake servers, and your guest book attendant, will also appreciate a small gift that expresses your thanks. Distribute the gifts before the wedding so you don't have to try to track down everyone after the honeymoon. The rehearsal dinner is a perfect time to give these gifts to your attendants.

Planning the Honeymoon

After all of the excitement and the flurry of activity surrounding your wedding day, you and your new husband are going to *need* a honeymoon. It'll be a time to relax, regroup, and just enjoy being with each other—alone and with no obligations or to-do lists. Even if you can't afford much, take at least a few days—even just a weekend—for this very special time in your lives.

The good news is: The groom plans the honeymoon— it's one wedding detail you don't have to worry about. Unless you trust his taste and judgment completely and absolutely, though, you may want to give a little input on where you'd like to go and what you want to do.

Arrangements for your honeymoon should be made as early as possible, especially if your wedding is during a peak month or you want to go to a popular location. Be aware that an off-peak wedding month may not necessarily be an off-peak vacation month. For example, March is one of the slower months for weddings, but it's also spring break for colleges across the United States. Beach towns and resorts will be crawling with college and university students whose primary goal is to see who can get the rowdiest, raunchiest, and drunkest. This may not be what you're looking for in a honeymoon.

If you want to leave the country for your honeymoon after a last minute wedding, make sure you have enough time to get a passport if you don't already have one. It takes a minimum of four to six weeks for a passport application to be processed. For information about obtaining a passport application in your area, look in the government pages of your phone book under *Postal Service*.

Consider working with a travel agent to plan your honeymoon. He or she can suggest destinations that you may not have thought of. An agent will also have inside information on travel bargains and can advise you on any special requirements, such as passports, shots, or paperwork you'll need to take care of.

Maybe you don't have the time, money, or desire to arrange a luxurious getaway on an exotic island paradise. But you can still have a great honeymoon without going halfway around the world or blowing a year's salary. You can stay in a nice hotel on the other side of town (or in a nearby town) that you rarely visit and where you're not likely to run into people you know. Eat at restaurants you've heard about but never tried and explore shops and sights you've never taken the time to seek out before. You and your new spouse can be just as alone in a crowd a few miles from home as you can on a private beach three time zones away.

Bridal Registries

Your wedding is one time in your life when your friends and loved ones will clamor to give you presents. You can make it easy for them (and hopefully discourage anyone from giving you a chartreuse and purple macramé wall hanging) by listing your needs and wants with a bridal registry.

Bridal registries are the ultimate wish list. They're offered as a free service by many stores and give you the opportunity to politely and discreetly tell others what you want. Here's how it works: Sometime in the process of planning your wedding (the earlier, the better), you and your future spouse can go to a store that offers a registry service and pick out the items you'd like to receive as gifts. The store will record your choices in its files and may even post its registry database on a Web site so you and those who want to buy you a gift can check the list from home. When family and friends go to the store to make a purchase, they can check your list and find something they know you'll like. The store keeps track of the purchases, which decreases your chances of receiving duplicates, and you can see at any time if you need to add more to the list or take some things off. Some chain stores network all of their bridal registries so that a person in, say, Seattle can pull up the wish list of a couple who registered at one of the chain's stores in San Antonio.

It used to be that couples listed only china, crystal, and silverware with bridal registries. But today you can register for practically anything. High-end department stores are still popular choices, but now mid-range department stores, import stores, and even some home improvement warehouse stores have gotten into the act and offer bridal registries. You can put everything from wooden spoons to bed sheets to wall clocks to table saws on your wish list.

Before you go nuts and run down to your favorite store, stop and think about what you want. Remember that the more you ask for, the greater the chance you'll have of getting a hodgepodge mixture of stuff. If your primary need or want is an entire set of china, for example, limit the choices you give your benefactors so they'll be more inclined to purchase the dishes.

You can register at more than one store if you'd like. Try to spread your list across a wide range of prices so that friends and family at all income levels will be able to find something on your list that they can afford.

Although bridal registries are a convenient and easy way to make your needs and wishes known, don't resort to guerrilla tactics to prod or shame people into filling your china cabinet and linen closet. You can register for crystal goblets and fuzzy bath mats if you like, but resist the temptation to cram your registry information down your friends' and relatives' throats. Tamara and Bob (names have been changed to protect the tacky) included a note about where they were registered *on their wedding invitations!* Stationing a muscle-bound guy named Vinnie by the front door of the wedding site to shake down guests as they entered would have been more subtle.

A far more dignified way to spread the word about your registry is by word-of-mouth. Pick up a handful of cards or brochures at your registry location and give one to anyone who asks what you need or want for your wedding. Many people will go to your mom and future mother-in-law for information on what you'd like, so make sure they have plenty of cards to hand out. And the person(s) who gives you a shower will want to include your registry information on the invitations she sends, so let her know as well.

Saying Thank You

Generally, the people you invite to your wedding are happy for you and they're going to express that happiness by giving you a gift. They may write out a check and put it in a wedding card filled with warmest wishes. Or they'll find out what you want or where you're registered and they'll traipse to the store to pick out that perfect little something they hope you'll like. They'll buy wrapping paper and tape and bows and a card, then they'll take it home and turn it into the prettiest package you ever saw. They'll take that gift with them when they get all dressed up to go to your wedding or they'll stand in line at the post office so they can send it to you in the mail.

You've got the easy part. All you have to do is open it and say thank you. Right about now, you're probably thinking, "Well, duh." But you'd be amazed at how many couples neglect the common courtesy of thanking people for gifts they receive. Don't be one of them.

Regardless of how small a gift people give you, remember that they went out of their way to do something nice for you. You may not like the gift they gave you—in fact, it may the ugliest thing on God's green earth—but they made an effort on your behalf and for that, you need to show your appreciation.

You can order thank you notes that match your invitations or pick up basic thank you notes at any card shop, stationery shop, office supply store, or department store. Notes with a generic, preprinted message inside are available, but many people will be offended if they receive one from you. And they've got a point. They went to the trouble of giving you a gift. A personal note of thanks two or three sentences long is not too much to ask in return.

Although you've got a million things to do in preparation for your wedding, try to write your thank you notes as you receive gifts. It won't take but a minute or two to write a simple note for one gift, and even the busiest bride- or groom-to-be can squeeze in a couple of notes each day. If you wait to write them all at once, you'll need a much larger block of time—and that may be hard to find.

Keep a record of every gift you receive—your wedding album should have several pages where you can list both the gifts and the givers. If your hostess hasn't already arranged it, ask someone to write down what everyone gives you at your shower(s). Don't open any gifts you receive by mail—including cards, which may have a check in them—until you have your list and a pen in front of you so you can record it immediately. Your fiancé should also keep track of gifts given to him so you can add them to your master list.

Write thank you notes for gifts you receive at the wedding as soon after returning from your honeymoon as possible. Most etiquette books say you have a year to get all of your thank you notes out, but don't wait that long. People expect you to thank them, and the longer you wait, the less they'll think of you. Be especially diligent about thanking people who send gifts by mail. They not only want to be thanked, but they need to know if you received their gift at all. You'll be mightily embarrassed when, six months after your wedding, cousin Jeanie in Des Moines calls to ask if you received the gift she mailed and you have to tell her yes, but you just haven't gotten around to thanking her yet.

Announcing Your Marriage

Although all of the most important people in your life will probably be at your wedding, there may be many more people you'd like to tell about your change in marital status. You have several options for getting the word out.

Last Minute Weddings

To let specific people know, you can send out announcements. Use the same style of card you chose for your wedding invitations, but order a set with slightly different wording. For example, instead of "so-and-so requests the honor of your presence at the marriage of...," change the inscription to "so-and-so has the honor of announcing the marriage of...." and so on. If you can find the time, have the announcements addressed, stamped, and ready to go by your wedding day and ask someone to drop them in a mailbox as you take off for your honeymoon. Be sure to keep your invitations and announcements separate as you address them so you don't get them mixed up and send the wrong ones to the wrong people.

For city- or county-wide coverage, put your announcement on your local newspaper's weddings and engagements page. Be sure to send in a photo with your write up, and check with the newspaper about getting your photo back after it's published. Some papers will return it to you by mail; others may require you to pick it up.

If you've got Web-literate friends and family around the country or the world, you can get the word out via the Internet. Several Web-based businesses will post your nuptial notice for up to a year, and the service is relatively inexpensive. (Of course, if you have the equipment and the ability, you can build and maintain your own site.) These services will create anything from a simple, text-only message on a wedding announcement page to an elaborate, photo-filled Web site that chronicles every little detail of your big day. Most of them offer package deals that include just about anything you can imagine: your scanned announcement/invitation, wedding and honeymoon photos, a written message from you, a link to your e-mail address, a guest book where visitors to your page can sign in and post their best wishes for you and your new spouse, a link to your online bridal registry, even an audio message from the two of you. Prices range from $50 for a three-month, 200-word, one-photo page to more than $300 for a 12-month, everything-but-the-kitchen-sink, password-protected extravaganza. Once your site is built, send an e-mail message to your friends and family announcing the address—they'll feel like the only part of your wedding they missed was trying to catch your bouquet. (See Appendix B for Web Wedding Announcement Sites.)

The things you'll be thinking about before your wedding will keep your head spinning for weeks. Picking out your wedding rings, planning showers and parties, buying attendants' gifts, planning your honeymoon, opening a bridal registry, saying thanks, and announcing your marriage are all the exciting things you will be doing even for the most last minute wedding.

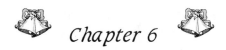

Chapter 6

Eloping—The Ultimate Last Minute Wedding

If you've flipped to this section of this book, you're probably either considering eloping or wondering what advice you could possibly need beyond "go to Vegas and find a chapel."

In this section, you're going to find the nitty gritty on how to pull off a great elopement. Where can you go? How do you get a marriage license? Do you make arrangements ahead of time or just take off? Can you invite people to come along? What do you wear? How much will it cost? If it concerns eloping, odds are good you're going to find the information here.

Eloping Pros and Cons

Eloping used to mean sneaking off in the middle of the night to get married in some cheesy wedding chapel with the romantic ambiance of a Taco Bell. It didn't matter what the real reasons were—if a couple eloped, everybody *knew* it was because they had gotten themselves into trouble.

Those days and attitudes are quickly disappearing as more and more couples are opting to turn their wedding into their own little romantic adventure. Eloping has become a very attractive alternative for tying the knot—

somewhere between the traditional white-lace-and-roses fairytale wedding and the lunch-hour trip to the justice of the peace.

Eloping has many advantages, but probably the biggest is that it allows you to indulge in your fantasies. Do you dream of exchanging vows in a tropical island paradise as hundreds of colorful butterflies circle overhead and a mountain waterfall cascades peacefully behind you? Maybe you fantasize about saying "I do" at the top of a snow-covered mountain or on a sailboat in the middle of a sparkling lake at sunset. Or perhaps you'd like nothing better than a traditional wedding ceremony, but in an intimate woodland chapel or lavishly landscaped rose garden. Eloping allows you to realize these dreams.

Although these fantasy weddings may sound completely out of reach, weddings like these really aren't just for people with trust funds and names like Skippy and Buffy. Taking your wedding on the road can cost significantly less than having a traditional ceremony and reception in your hometown. When you elope, you save on everything from invitations and decorations to wedding favors and butter mints.

Wedding service providers and chapels around the country offer wedding packages at a fraction of the cost of the typical traditional wedding and reception. You can pay anywhere from less than $200 for a simple ceremony in a historic mansion in the Ozarks to several thousand dollars for a deluxe, anything-your-heart-desires wedding and honeymoon package in Hawaii. And because a good number of wedding service providers are set up in exotic or vacation locations, you can combine your wedding and honeymoon and reduce your costs even more.

As an added bonus—there's virtually no stress. Places that specialize in marrying eloping couples take care of all the details for you. You choose the options you want: photographer, cake, flowers, champagne toast, and they'll make sure you get it. Some will even provide a limo to take you the courthouse to get a marriage license and rent traditional wedding attire for both you and your fiancé.

Eloping can save wear-and-tear on your wallet and your blood pressure, and it can also provide the perfect solution to some problem situations. For instance, it may be an especially attractive option if the wedding you're planning is not your first. Kim and Phil had both been married before and had lived together for two years when they decided to get married. Given their situation, a big church wedding seemed a bit silly, but they still wanted the official joining of their lives to be special. They took a couple days off from work, drove a few hours out of town, and got married in a charming mountain wedding chapel. For them, it was much more fun, memorable, and sensible than a traditional wedding.

Difficult family situations can also make eloping a good choice. If you have dueling in-laws or your divorced parents make life miserable when they're within striking distance of each other, eloping can save you a lot of headache, heartache, and embarrassment. And if you've lost someone special, eloping can make this person's absence from your wedding less painful. Corrina's father died a year before she and Kevin decided to get married. Corrina couldn't bear the thought of anyone else walking her down the aisle, so she and Kevin eloped to Lake Tahoe for an intimate and personal wedding.

Eloping has a lot of advantages, but there are also some potential problems you should at least consider before you hop on the plane. The most obvious problem—and probably the thorniest—is the other people in your lives. Eloping doesn't necessarily mean excluding the people who are most important to you. If you want to bring family or friends along to share your moment, most wedding service providers are more than happy to accommodate them (see "To Tell or Not to Tell?" later in this chapter). But what if you don't want anyone else to join your wedding party? You should do what you feel is right for you and your situation, but realize that you may be sailing on some pretty rough water when you return home and those closest to you find out about your elopement.

Another potential downside is only a problem if you're counting on mountains of wedding gifts. Unless they're really close to you or they're invited to some event in celebration of your marriage, most people won't feel an obligation (or even remember, for that matter) to give a gift to a couple whose wedding they didn't attend. But many couples figure that a reduction in the number of gifts they receive is a small price to pay for the stress-free, intimate wedding they are able to have by eloping. (You can sidestep this problem by having a wedding reception when your return. See page 90.)

Planned or Spontaneous?

Personalities, both yours and your fiancé's, will play a role in the type of elopement you decide on. If you're the spontaneous type, you might want to hop on a plane and head to a town that you know has several wedding chapels, find one you like the looks of, and walk right in. A more deliberate, methodical couple may prefer to choose the perfect spot, make all of the arrangements ahead of time, and know exactly what to expect once they get there.

If you're of the fly-by-the-seat-of-your-pants variety, a few words of advice: Be flexible—things may not turn out exactly as you expect. The only preparations Brenda and Brian made for their wedding were plane tickets and hotel reservations. Once they arrived in Las Vegas, they found they weren't the only couple who thought April Fool's Day was the perfect time to get married. Every chapel they tried had long waiting lines, so they went back to their hotel to come up with a Plan B. Flipping through a what-to-do-in-Vegas magazine, they found a company specializing in airborne weddings. One call and 30 minutes later, they exchanged vows in a helicopter circling above The Strip. Everything worked out fine in the end because they were willing to adjust to the situation.

Unless you're going someplace like Las Vegas, Lake Tahoe, Maui, Gatlinburg, or Eureka Springs that has several options for spur-of-the-moment weddings, consider at least calling ahead of time to make sure the location of your choice accepts walk-ins and will be open for business. The last thing you want is to travel to Monroe, Georgia, only to find out that the sole wedding chapel in town is closed for the weekend so the proprietor can attend Aunt Martha's funeral in Topeka.

Appendix B, with a list of more than 70 wedding chapels, will get you started in your search for the perfect place for your elopement, whether it's planned or spontaneous. Also, you can check out www.quickwed.com, where you'll find an extensive database listing some 2,000 wedding service providers and wedding chapels in the United States. If you don't have Internet access, go to the library and look through phone books of places you might like to go to elope. If there are any in that area, the yellow pages will list them under *Wedding Chapels and Ceremonies* or *Wedding Supplies and Services,* or something similar.

To Tell or Not to Tell?

The timing for announcing your elopement can be a tricky thing. If yours is a spur-of-the-moment elopement, simple logistics can dictate a post-wedding announcement. If, on the other hand, you opt for a planned elopement and have plenty of time to tell everyone before the big day, you have a big decision to make.

Although you're thrilled and excited about your upcoming adventure, some of your friends or relatives may feel hurt at being left out of the festivities. In fact, unless you have a very rare circle of family and friends, you can count on people trying to talk you out of eloping (especially if you plan to go without them). That can make you feel guilty and add a tremendous amount of stress to what should be a blissful, carefree, and romantic experience. If you're absolutely set on eloping and there's an inkling of a chance that someone whose opinion is important to you will slip a disc over your plans, keep quiet. You know that saying that says it's easier to ask for forgiveness than permission? It applies here.

That said, it's also true that there's no rule that says guests can't be included in an elopement. There may be some people in your life who you are sure will hold a serious grudge against you until the day they're put in the ground if they're not asked to be a part of your wedding. In a case like this, you may want to consider inviting them to join you. But think before you ask. Guests can complicate things a bit, so make sure you think it through before you ask anyone to come along.

Let's assume you're eloping so you and your new spouse can spend a few intimate, idyllic days relaxing and enjoying each other's company. If you invite guests to witness your nuptials, you may feel you have to include them in your honeymoon activities—after all, they *did* come all that way just for you. You may feel like you're responsible for making sure they're entertained and happy and before you know it, your intimate, idyllic days can slip away.

Last Minute Weddings

When Jenny and Marc told a few people about their plans to elope, their guest list quickly spun out of control—they ended up with an entourage of 40 when they married in Eureka Springs. Their main objective in eloping was to simplify their wedding—instead they became social directors for a weekend. A few months later, they took a cruise—alone—to make up for the privacy and intimacy they missed out on during their wedding weekend.

On the other hand, your philosophy on eloping may be "the more, the merrier." Brandie and Don invited their parents, siblings, and grandparents along when they eloped to Lake Tahoe and married on a cruise ship. After the ceremony, the wedding party spent the evening dining and dancing as the boat cruised across the moonlit lake. Over the next few days, they gambled in the casinos and took in the local sights together—and had a blast.

Whatever your opinion concerning guests is, be sure you and your mate are on the same page. You don't want to let a guest list—or the lack of one—spoil your wedding trip.

So, let's say you decide that inviting a few of your loved ones would add the perfect touch to your wedding—who foots the bill? If you're loaded and really want your friends and/or family to join you, you can offer to pay their way. (Notice that's "can," and not "must" or "should.") If you're like most of us, though, and can't or don't want to pay your guests' way, don't feel bad about not offering.

Look at it this way: If you asked another couple to join you for dinner at a restaurant, you wouldn't feel obligated to pick up the tab for them, would you? You could if you wanted to, but no one would think any less of you if you didn't offer.

It's the same with inviting friends or family to your elopement. Your guests, in addition to watching you pledge your love to each other, will get a little vacation or at least a weekend away when they join in your wedding party. And if they can't or don't want to shell out the money to follow you to your wedding destination, they can simply decline the invitation.

Which leads us to what could be a down side to eloping. When you make the decision to marry at a far-away site, you have to accept the fact that some or all of those you invite may not be able to make it. If it's terribly important that certain people attend your wedding and they've indicated that they're not willing or able to travel to it, you might want to offer to pay their way or rethink your plans to elope. You have to decide what's more important to you—eloping or including loved ones in your wedding.

Organizing Your Elopement

Once you decide to go for it, fantasies and daydreams play a vital role in helping you decide where you'll go to get married. But a couple of other, more down-to-earth factors, such as time and money, should be considered, too. You may see two weeks of sun, palm trees, and exotic love scenes on a tropical beach as your destiny, but if you can scrape together only $50 between the two of you, chances are good that Maui's not a realistic choice.

Budgeting money for your elopement

Before you get all wrapped up in choosing your wedding site, set a budget. Think about what your checkbook looks like now and what your financial needs will be after you return home from your trip. A spare-no-expense getaway to Maui is great for those couples who can afford it, but the luster will quickly wear off your memories if you have to decide between paying your wedding trip bills and buying groceries. Set your budget at a realistic level, then go from there.

Following a budget doesn't mean you'll have to settle for a wedding in some dive joint decorated with velvet paintings, plastic flowers, and purple shag carpet. Let's go back to the sun and palm tree fantasy. Maybe your budget won't accommodate Maui, but how about a similar location that's a bit more manageable? California, Texas, Florida, and South Carolina are just a few states that have great beach resorts *and* wedding chapels. A week or two—even a weekend—at one of these places can be just as magical and romantic as Maui, and your memories will be sweeter knowing that your fantasy wedding didn't throw you into a financial pit you'll never climb out of.

Budgeting time for your elopement

Once you've decided how much money you can spend, figure out how much time you can take for your wedding trip and how long you have to plan it.

Is a long weekend about all you can spare for your romantic adventure? Then choose a location that's easy to get to. When your time is limited, you don't want to waste precious hours with complicated flight schedules or day-long drives. Or can you and your future mate afford the luxury of a couple of weeks for your wedding trip? Then a location that's harder to get to will take a proportionately smaller chunk of your time and might even make the whole adventure more enjoyable. Say you choose a secluded cabin in the mountains—a day's drive from your home. The trip there can build the excitement and anticipation for your upcoming nuptials, while the drive home can help you gradually make the transition from the fantasy world you just left to the everyday life you're about to reenter.

How much time do you have to plan your wedding? Some wedding service providers require reservations up to a month ahead of time. Others just ask for a day or two's notice or don't require a heads-up at all. Be aware that if you plan to marry on a lovers' holiday (Valentine's Day, New Year's Eve, or even April Fools Day) or a holiday weekend (Memorial Day, the 4th of July, or Labor Day), you're going to run into much bigger crowds than at other times of the year. If you're determined to get married at one of the high-traffic times, get your reservations in as far ahead of time as possible or have a list of alternate locations ready in case your first choice doesn't pan out.

Also consider how you'll get to your wedding location when you're making your choice. If you want to get married right away, you'll probably want to pick a location within close driving distance. For locations beyond driving distance, give yourself more planning time. Airfares are generally lower when you can make reservations a couple of weeks in advance. If that's not possible, check into some of the airline ticket buying services on the Internet (listed in Appendix B). With a little flexibility, you can get to the place you want to go and save some money at the same time.

Wedding Service Providers

Once you decide on a location for your elopement, take a few minutes to check up on your wedding service provider of choice. Because you'll be making your arrangements long distance, you should start with a call to the Better Business Bureau and/or the chamber of commerce in the area to see if any complaints have been filed against the provider. Then, if you get the all-clear, call the provider and ask for references. You'll also want to get as much information on the service as possible—knowing

Last Minute Weddings

what to expect before you get there can save time, money, and frustration on your wedding day. Here are some questions you may want to ask:

- ✓ Can you obtain a marriage license and/or rings from the provider?
- ✓ Does the provider have wedding attire available for both the bride and groom to rent?
- ✓ Does the provider charge extra if you bring guests?
- ✓ Can the provider arrange a small reception if you choose to have guests attend your wedding?
- ✓ Can the provider arrange for a photographer and/or videographer?
- ✓ Will you be charged extra if you have a guest take pictures or videos instead of using the provider's photographer?
- ✓ What type of photos (35mm glossy prints, Polaroid instant snapshots, etc.) does the provider offer?
- ✓ Do you get custody of the negatives or does the photographer retain them?
- ✓ Does the provider offer any wedding/honeymoon packages?

When you find a wedding service provider you like, find out what kind of reservations, if any, are required. In general, wedding service providers who require reservations ask that you make them anywhere from one day to one month in advance, although some very popular locations fill up quickly and you may need to make your call farther in advance. These providers also tend to require full or partial payment up front.

Out-of-the-Ordinary Elopements

Eloping allows you to let your hair down and have the kind of wedding you want. If you don't want a traditional wedding in a chapel, then don't have one.

Maybe you want to exchange your vows on the mountaintop in Colorado where your fiancé proposed to you, or under the oak tree in Connecticut where you shared your first kiss. Or maybe you like the idea of getting hitched on horseback and riding off into the sunset with your beloved. This kind of wedding may take a little more work on your part, but you certainly have that wedding of your dreams.

Many officiants—ministers, judges, etc.—will go just about anywhere to perform your out-of-the-ordinary marriage ceremony. Most are available on very short notice and are on call 24 hours a day. If the officiant has to travel to your wedding site, plan on paying that expense in addition to the regular fee. Also remember that you'll most likely have to make your own arrangements for flowers, photographer, witnesses (if necessary), and any other accouterments you'd like. You can find an officiant by looking in the phone book of the nearest city under *Wedding Chapels and Ceremonies* or some variation.

Some resorts in exotic locales such as Jamaica and the Bahamas offer complimentary or low-cost wedding packages if you honeymoon with them. These wedding/honeymoon packages should be booked four to six months in advance, especially during peak wedding season. Packages include things like champagne, flowers, and breakfast in bed the day after the wedding and you can choose from several locations to exchange your vows. Many of these resorts are all-inclusive; everything—meals, drinks, activities, and entertainment—is included in the price of your honeymoon package.

Last Minute Weddings

When planning an out-of-the-ordinary elopement, keep in mind the interests and abilities you both share. You can make your wedding unique simply by choosing a special place or incorporating an activity you're *both* comfortable with. That's not to say you shouldn't do anything wild and exciting—just make sure you're both up to it, physically and mentally.

Getting a Marriage License

Marriage license requirements are something you should think about before you elope to some distant place. While many states require nothing more than cash and a driver's license to issue an on-the-spot marriage license, some states, like Indiana and Nebraska, require medical examinations before you can receive a license. In other states, including Texas and Maine, couples must wait a mandated period of time between obtaining a license and getting married. And some states, such as Minnesota and Georgia, issue licenses that are valid only in the county where they're purchased, not the entire state.

You can start on your quest for marriage license information by calling a wedding service provider. Because marrying couples is their business, they'll be able to give you all the particulars for getting a license in their area. If you're not using a wedding service provider, get in touch with the county courthouse where you're thinking of having your wedding. Another option is to check state requirements on the Internet. Use a search engine like Infoseek or Yahoo and do a keyword search using the name of the state and the word "weddings." You'll get a whole list of sites that give requirements for that state. But beware: Requirements can and do change, yet Web sites aren't always updated to reflect the changes. Use the information you get from these sites as a starting place, but be sure to call the county courthouse or a wedding service provider to verify that the information is correct.

If you plan to get married on a cruise or at a resort outside of the country, marriage license requirements may be very different from those for couples marrying in the United States. For example, you may have to arrive a few days before your wedding because some resorts are in countries that have residency requirements of up to several days. Your travel agent or the resort wedding coordinator will be able to give you information about obtaining a marriage license and the legalities of marrying out of the country.

What to Wear

In the grand scheme of things, what you wear to elope may seem a pretty trivial matter. After all, you're setting off on a romantic adventure that will forever change the course of your life. What difference does it make if you're wearing designer fashions or a burlap sack?

Plenty, as a matter of fact. Your clothes can make an occasion special and memorable—two feelings you probably want to associate with your wedding day. Even if you don't care for an elaborate gown and a tuxedo, take a little time and effort to choose your wedding outfits.

Tiffany didn't think much about what she'd wear when she and Mike exchanged their vows, but once she got to the chapel, she wished she had. In her haphazardly chosen green dress, she felt more like she was strolling into the office than walking down the aisle. Three years later, her choice of clothing remains her only regret about eloping.

For information about how and where to buy a traditional wedding dress in a hurry, turn to Chapter 2. If you want to wear a traditional wedding dress but don't want to go to the expense of buying one, you might be able to rent one from the resort, chapel, etc. Call and ask.

On the other hand, a traditional wedding dress may be the last thing you want to get married in. After all, you're eloping so you're not bound by anyone's expectations about what to do or wear. You might think a cocktail dress and sparkly earrings are more "you" than a traditional white gown and pearls. Maybe you'd be more comfortable in something with less razzle-dazzle, like a suit or a nice dress.

To find your perfect, nontraditional wedding outfit, check the selection at higher-end department stores and dress shops in your area. Outlet stores offer a nice variety as well (but be careful—many carry second-quality and/or irregular merchandise). Department store catalogs are another option, and most have liberal return policies if you don't like the dress once you see it in person.

Another nontraditional option is to dress in keeping with the theme of your wedding location. For example, a wedding at a dude ranch in Wyoming might send you to a western clothing store for boots and a western-style wedding dress. Perhaps you're planning to tie the knot on the beach in Antigua or Jamaica. Consider going native and buying an outfit in the local style once you arrive.

Some wedding chapels take the theme idea even farther. In Las Vegas, you can have an intergalactic ceremony in a starship chapel or a Blue Hawaii wedding complete with hula girls and a singing Elvis as your officiant. With a day's notice, a provider can even arrange for appropriate costumes for you so you don't have to worry about finding outfits that will complement the theme.

Packing for Elopement

If you're eloping by plane, pack your wedding outfits and anything else you absolutely must have when you exchange vows in carry-on luggage. Flight attendants on larger planes are generally more than happy to help you find a safe home for your wedding dress if you ask. But if you take a smaller plane or a shuttle, you may be on your own. So bring your dress on board with you and put it in a safe place where you can keep an eye on it, making sure it doesn't get squashed under someone's backpack.

Why all the fuss about carrying your wedding outfits on the plane with you? Murphy's Law dictates that if you pack your gown in your suitcase, a baggage guy with a hangover will run a forklift through your Samsonite as he prepares to load it on a plane that's heading somewhere you're not. This is not the kind of wedding memory you want to have.

Another option is to ship your wedding dress ahead of time to the hotel you'll be staying in. Call the hotel manager before you mail it, though, to be sure he or she will accept it and keep it in a safe place until you arrive. Also ask if the hotel supplies an iron or an ironing service. If not, bring an iron with you.

When the Honeymoon Is Over

You're back in town. The wedding was great; the honeymoon was even better. Now what?

You may not have taken the traditional path to the altar, but you and your husband are still newlyweds. Act like it! Tell the world. Throw a party. Celebrate and share this very special time in your lives with those you love.

Announcing your marriage

If you didn't inform those closest to you about your plans beforehand, you'll probably want to call or tell them face to face now. Don't be surprised if a few friends or

Last Minute Weddings

loved ones are shocked and even a little upset when they first hear about your change in marital status. But unless they truly despise the person you married, they'll see that you're happy and will eventually be happy for you.

You can let others (such as your extended family and friends who live a long-distance call away) know about your wedding by sending them an announcement or personal note. If you plan to have a reception, your announcement can pull double duty and act as an invitation as well (more on post-wedding receptions later in this chapter). Chapter 3 contains everything you need to know about wedding invitations—you can easily use that information when you start putting your announcements together. Whether you want them to be formal, casual, or somewhere in-between, there are so many options to choose from that you're sure to find announcements to fit your taste and budget.

You can use the same style of announcement that most couples select for traditional wedding invitations, but you'll need to adjust the wording to reflect your situation. Instead of the customary "Mr. and Mrs. So-and-So and Mr. and Mrs. This-and-That request the honor of your presence at the marriage of their children, blah, blah, blah...," include a few details about your elopement—when, where, and how. You can use traditional-type wording, or have fun with it and make up your own inscription.

If you're the creative type, you could spread your news in poem or verse. Remember, though, that traditional announcements/invitations have only a limited amount of space that can be printed on, so compose a short verse, not a long-winded epic.

You can season your announcement with a touch of your personality. Cindy and Steve chose a formal design for the announcement/invitation they sent out. Instead of traditional wording, though, they came up with an inscription that reflected the sense of fun and adventure that surrounded their elopement. Adorned with embossed roses and printed in a dainty, elegant script, the front of their announcement read, "Oops! They eloped...." Inside, they gave a few details and invited recipients to share in their happiness at a reception. The announcement not only got the word out, but it also set the tone for the party that would follow.

Another announcement idea is to share a bit of the place where you got married with your friends and family. Buy a stack of picture postcards at your wedding location and send them out with the news of your change in marital status once you return home. If you plan to throw a reception or party using your wedding location as the theme, the postcards will make great invitations. Be sure to save one to put in your wedding keepsake book.

Don't forget to announce your nuptials on the social page of your local newspaper—it's not just for couples who had traditional weddings. Be sure to send in a photo with your write-up, especially if you eloped to some exotic or unusual location. The photo of you and your groom wearing leis or standing at the top of a snow-covered mountain will be the first one people notice as they scan the page full of brides and grooms in lacy gowns and black tuxedos. See Chapter 5 for complete information on putting your announcement in the paper and on other ways to get the word out about your marriage.

Gifts and registries

When you return home from your wedding trip, your friends and loved ones may want to honor you and your new mate with a bridal shower or two. And if you have a reception, most of your friends will come with wedding gifts in tow. Make it easy for them to choose the perfect gift by filling out your wish list with a bridal registry in your favorite store(s). Chapter 5 covers bridal registries in detail, but because you're doing things backwards, you'll need to make some special arrangements.

Most registries will keep your list on file for six months after your wedding date. But depending on the type of reception you have, you might not even send out announcements until a month after your wedding, and your reception may be six weeks after that. Before you know it, half of your time could be used up. Explain your situation to the bridal registry consultant—in most cases, she'll adjust the time limit and keep your list in the registry for six months after the reception date.

The post-elopement reception

A reception can give family and friends a chance to celebrate your marriage with you once you return home from your trip. You can throw the party yourself, or you can accept a loved one's offer to host it. If many of your friends or family are unacquainted with your new spouse or family, a post-elopement party can be a good way for everyone to get to know each other. It may also smooth the ruffled feathers of those who felt snubbed because they weren't included in your elopement. And if some loved ones are *really* upset about being left out of your wedding, allowing them to play a part in planning your reception may help cool them down. (Be careful with this, though. A hurt or ticked-off person on your planning committee can use guilt to manipulate you, adding a lot of stress to what should be a fun finale to your eloping experience.)

The same free-spirited approach you took with your elopement can guide you in planning your reception. You can throw a black-tie affair at the country club or a shorts-and-tank-top picnic in the backyard. Invite everyone in town or just a few close friends. Spend weeks planning every intricate detail or call the gang over for an impromptu blowout. The details are all up to you. You've already dashed traditional expectations by eloping, so don't worry now about doing the "right" thing.

Obviously, the amount of preparation and planning you'll have to do for your reception depends on how elaborate a party you want. A casual bash can come together in a matter of a week or two while a big, formal gathering could take a couple of months to orchestrate. Before you embark on your journey to create a grand and glorious soiree, though, realize that if you had married in a traditional wedding, at least half of your planning and expense would have been for the reception. In other words, organizing the reception can become as complicated, stressful, and costly as planning the big wedding you avoided by eloping.

Chapter 4 covers the nuts and bolts of organizing a reception for a traditional wedding. The information and advice you'll find there can also apply to a post-elopement reception. The sections "Choosing Your Location" in Chapter 1 and "The Photographer/Videographer" in Chapter 2 offer planning advice you'll find useful as well.

Because your reception is a celebration of your marriage, consider incorporating some traditional wedding customs into the festivities. Wear your wedding outfits, throw a bouquet, toss a garter, offer toasts, serve wedding cake, have the first dance with your new husband. Make sure to bring along your wedding photos and/or video so everyone can share in your exciting, romantic adventure. (You can help loved ones who aren't able to travel to your reception—especially your older relatives—feel like they're still a part of the celebration by sending them a copy of your wedding video and photos.)

Last Minute Weddings

Think about using your wedding location as the theme for your reception. If you eloped to Hawaii, throw a luau complete with leis, seashells, and tropical drinks topped with little paper umbrellas. A rose-garden wedding could inspire you to hold your reception in a gazebo or a friend's beautifully landscaped backyard, and a western wedding just begs for a barbecue and country music.

If you really want to cause a stir when you tell people you've eloped, don't tell them at all. Keep your elopement a secret even after you return home and then throw a party. Once guests arrive and things are humming along, direct everyone's attention to the TV screen and show your wedding video without giving any clues about what they're watching. It won't take long for your guests to realize what's happening, and their shrieks of delight at your surprise announcement will add the perfect closing touch to your eloping adventure.

There's no doubt that the word "elope" means different things to different couples. You can sneak out your bedroom window or you can plan the whole thing with family and friends in attendance. But however you arrange the logistics, you and your new mate can look to your future with hope, happiness, and love.

Chapter 7

Summary

Remember the young woman from Chapter 1, the one I stepped on in the bookstore? I never saw her again, so I don't know how her wedding turned out or if she managed to keep her sanity as she put it together. But I do know that the advice I gave her is the same advice I'd give to anyone who's feeling overwhelmed at the thought of planning a wedding, regardless of how much time they have: Relax, don't panic, and enjoy yourself.

Whenever you're feeling stressed, frustrated, or like you need to be doing a dozen different things at the same time, step back and take a deep breath. Do you really think anyone will care if you don't have wedding programs or if your bridesmaids aren't wearing identical shoes? Will it ruin everything if your florist doesn't have enough time to order lilies and you have to use roses or daisies instead? Will your guests walk out in disgust if you skip the wedding favors or offer cake and punch instead of a full meal at the reception?

Don't allow the pressure to create the "perfect" wedding drive you crazy and transform you from your normal self into a grouchy hot-head no one wants to be around. Your wedding is your day to celebrate the love you and your fiancé have for each other and to share that love with those you care about. If you're looking at your wedding as something you can't wait to get over with because planning it is such a miserable, painful experience, maybe you're focusing on what's expected of you and not on what's important to you. Make your wedding what you want it to be—if it's right for you and your husband-to-be, it's right.

Whether you're planning to have an elaborate traditional wedding in your hometown, exchange your vows in the presence of a few friends in your backyard, or elope to parts unknown, relax and try not to sweat the small stuff. You want your strongest wedding-day memories to be the look on his face as you walk down the aisle and the feelings you have as you pledge your eternal love to each other, not the relief you feel when the wedding is finally over.

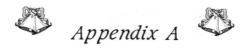

Appendix A

Wedding Timeline

If you have six months to plan

Six months before the wedding
- ✓ Pick a date.
- ✓ Set your budget.
- ✓ Choose location(s) for your wedding and reception.
- ✓ Determine who will be in your wedding.

Five months before the wedding
- ✓ Line up your officiant.
- ✓ Buy or order your wedding gown.
- ✓ Select your wedding colors and bridesmaids' dresses.
- ✓ Find out marriage license requirements.
- ✓ Interview and book photographer and/or videographer.
- ✓ Start making honeymoon plans.

Four months before the wedding
- ✓ Put together invitation list.
- ✓ Order invitations.
- ✓ Select caterer and menu.
- ✓ Book band or DJ.

Last Minute Weddings

Three months before the wedding
✓ Select and reserve men's attire.
✓ Select florist and decorations.
✓ Select baker and order wedding cake.
✓ Register for gifts.
✓ Buy wedding rings.

Two months before the wedding
✓ Address invitations and mail four to six weeks before the wedding.
✓ Order wedding accessories (favors, unity candle, garter, cameras, etc.).
✓ Reserve rental equipment needed for the wedding and/or reception.
✓ Choose music for the wedding.

One month before the wedding
✓ Make appointment for hair and nails on wedding day.
✓ Buy and wrap gifts for wedding party.
✓ Get marriage license.
✓ Plan rehearsal dinner.
✓ Finalize honeymoon plans.

One week before the wedding
✓ Call all vendors to confirm wedding date, time, and place.
✓ Arrange name change on bank accounts, driver's license, credit and social security cards.
✓ Pack for honeymoon.

Wedding day
✓ Go to hair and nail appointment.
✓ Relax and give yourself plenty of time to get dressed.

If you have three months to plan

Three months before the wedding

- ✓ Pick a date.
- ✓ Set your budget.
- ✓ Choose location(s) for your wedding and reception.
- ✓ Determine who will be in your wedding.
- ✓ Buy or order your wedding gown.
- ✓ Book photographer and/or videographer.
- ✓ Line up your officiant.

Two months before the wedding

- ✓ Select your wedding colors and bridesmaids' dresses.
- ✓ Start making honeymoon plans.
- ✓ Put together invitation list.
- ✓ Order invitations.
- ✓ Select caterer and menu.
- ✓ Book band or DJ.
- ✓ Select florist and decorations.

Six weeks before the wedding

- ✓ Find out marriage license requirements.
- ✓ Address invitations and mail four to six weeks before wedding.
- ✓ Select and reserve men's attire.
- ✓ Select baker and order wedding cake.

Last Minute Weddings

One month before the wedding

✓ Register for gifts.
✓ Buy wedding rings.
✓ Order wedding accessories (favors, unity candle, garter, cameras, etc.).
✓ Reserve rental equipment needed for wedding and/or reception.
✓ Choose music for wedding.

Three weeks before the wedding

✓ Get marriage license.
✓ Plan rehearsal dinner.
✓ Buy and wrap gifts for wedding party.

Two weeks before the wedding

✓ Make appointment for hair and nails on wedding day.
✓ Finalize honeymoon plans.
One week before the wedding
✓ Call all vendors to confirm wedding date, time, and place.
✓ Arrange name change on bank accounts, driver's license, credit and social security cards.
✓ Pack for honeymoon.

Wedding day

✓ Go to hair and nail appointment.
✓ Relax and give yourself plenty of time to get dressed.

Wedding Worksheet

Wedding date and time: _____

Budget: _____

	Estimated	Actual
Bridal gown		
Accessories		
Groom's tuxedo		
Bride's rings		
Groom's rings		
Attendants' attire		
Photography		
Videography		
Ceremony musicians		
Reception entertainment		
Wedding cake		
Flowers		
Additional ceremony decorations		
Food/beverage/catering		
Ceremony facility		
Reception facility		
Officiant		
Hair/makeup		
Transportation		
Rental equipment		
Wedding license		
Attendants' gifts		
Gifts for each other		
Honeymoon		

Last Minute Weddings

Wedding location
Place _____

Phone _____

Contact person _____

Reception location
Place _____

Phone _____

Contact person _____

Officiant
Name _____

Phone _____

Counseling schedule, if required (dates and times)

_____

_____

_____

License
Date to apply _____

Requirements _____

Dress
Store _____

Phone _____

Consultant _____

Description _____

Date ordered _____

Date promised _____

Fitting/alteration appointments

_____

_____

_____

Photographer and videographer

Photographer _____

Phone _____

Videographer _____

Phone _____

Wedding colors _____

Attendants' outfits

Store _____

Phone _____

Descriptions _____

Price _____

Date ordered _____

Date promised _____

Invitations and other stationery

Store _____

Phone _____

Salesperson _____

Date ordered _____

Date promised _____

Style #s for:

Invitations _____

Announcements _____

RSVP cards _____

Thank you notes _____

Extras

Mementos _____

Programs _____

Last Minute Weddings

Flowers and decorations

Florist _____

Phone _____

Salesperson _____

Date ordered _____

Date and time of delivery _____

Description _____

_____

Other decorations

_____

_____

Music

Ceremony musicians _____

Name _____

Phone _____

Arrival and departure times _____ / _____

Music selections:

Preceding ceremony

_____

_____

_____

_____

_____

Processional _____

Solos and music during ceremony

_____

_____

_____

_____

Recessional _____

Reception entertainment

Name _____

Phone _____

Arrival and departure times _____ / _____

Rehearsal and dinner

Arrival time at wedding location _____

Restaurant/caterer _____

Phone _____

Contact person _____

Date _____

Time _____

Food, drinks, caterer

Phone _____

Contact person _____

Menu:

Hors d'oeuvers _____

_____

_____

Entrée (choice of) _____

_____

_____

Type of service _____

Wedding Cake

Bakery _____

Phone _____

Salesperson _____

Delivery time _____

Last Minute Weddings

Rental equipment

Store _____

Phone _____

Salesperson _____

Items to reserve _____

_____

_____

Deliver and setup date/time _____ / _____

Pickup date/time_____ / _____

Rings

Jeweler _____

Phone _____

Salesperson _____

Engraving _____

Promised date for pickup _____

Honeymoon

Location _____

Phone _____

Agent _____

Departure and arrival dates_____ / _____

Ticket and flight numbers _____

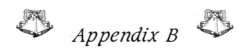

Appendix B

Wedding Resource List

Bridal and bridesmaids' dresses

America's Bridal Discounters
Name-brand wedding gowns and bridesmaids' dresses
discounted at least 30percent. Send or call with
manufacturer's name and style number or page number from
a bridal magazine for a price quote.
www.bridalgallery.com/bridaldiscounters/
1-800-326-0833

Chadwick's of Boston Special Occasions Catalog
Order bridesmaids' dresses at same time to insure same dye
lot and colors.
1-800-525-6650

JCPenney Bridal Catalog
www.jcpenney.com
1-800-527-8347

Sears Roebuck
Smart Choice (sizes 4-18) or Woman's View (sizes 18-56)
catalogs contain special-occasion dresses.
www.sears.com/specat/fashcat.htm

Spiegel
Catalog carries special occasion dresses and some wedding
ring sets (cubic zirconia only).
www.spiegel.com
1-800-527-1577

Invitations, wedding favors, decorations

Ann's Wedding Stationery
1-800-821-7011

Camelot Wedding Stationery and Accessories
1-800-280-2860

Creations by Elaine
1-800-452-4593

Evangel Christian Wedding Invitations
1-800-457-9774

Invitations by Dawn
1-800-332-3296

It's Your Wedding by Rexcraft
1-888-796-1184

Jamie Lee Fine Wedding Stationery
1-800-288-5800

Now & Forever Wedding Invitations & Accessories
1-800-521-0584 or 1-800-451-0610

Rexcraft
1-800-635-3898

The Precious Collection
1-800-537-5222

Wedding Traditions by Sugar n' Spice
1-800-535-1002

Willow Tree Lane
1-800-219-1022

Specialty papers/invitation kits

Paper Access
www.paperaccess.com/
1-800-727-3701

Paper Direct
www.paperdirect.com/
1-800-APAPERS

The Wedding Store
www.wedguide.com/store/

Ultimate Wedding Store
www.ultimatewedding.com/store/

Wedmart.com
www.wedmart.com
1-888-802-2229

Flowers

Roses by 2G
www.freshroses.com
1-800-880-0735

Rittner's Floral School Floral Education Center
Step-by-step instructions for making floral arrangements.
www.tiac.net/users/stevrt/RittnersGallery.html

Wedding accessories

(All catalogs under Invitations *also carry wedding accessories.)*

Affectionately Yours
www.affectionately-yours.com

Bridalink Store
www.bridalink.com/store2/

The Sarina Collection
www.sarinacollection.com/
1-888-6SARINA

The Wedding Helpers
www.weddinghelpers.com/
1-800-274-0675 or (714) 281-5013

Last Minute Weddings

The Wedding Shopper
www.theweddingshopper.com/catalog.htm

The Wedding Store
www.wedguide.com/store/

Treasured Moments
www.treasured-moments.com/
1-800-754-5151

Ultimate Wedding Store
www.ultimatewedding.com/store/

Wedding World Store
www.wedding-world.com/

Wedmart.com
www.wedmart.com
1-888-802-2229

WedNet Store
www.wednet.com/store/

Cake toppers and servers

All in Chocolate
Wedding chocolates including favors and cake toppers.
www.chocolatelady.com/wedding.htm
1-800-4CANDY3

Courtney Wedding Chocolates
Personalized candy wedding favors. Call for catalog.
1-800-323-0789

Creative Chocolates
www.creativechocolates.com/wedding.html
(210) 824-2462

Phillips Candy House
Wedding chocolates including favors and cake toppers
www.bostonchocolate.com/wedding.html
1-800-722-0905

The Wedding Center
Wedding favors you can assemble. Call for catalog.
(916) 424-5612

Wilton Online Catalog
www.weddingcake.com/wilton%20catalog/
Wiltonhomepage.html
1-800-850-7763

Wedding cameras

Best Camera
1-888-237-8226

Boecks Camera
1-800-700-5090

EPP Wedding Products
www.perfect-wedding.com/safari.html
(412) 823-6748

Catering

How to Cater Your Own Wedding Reception
www.chefmike.com
(770) 565-8865

Jeanne's Wedding Information Page
www.mindspring.com/~thinds/jmh/wedinfo.htm

Bridal registries

Bloomingdales
www.bloomingdales.com
(877) 888-2WED

Club Wedd at Target
www.target.com/
1-800-888-9333

Last Minute Weddings

Dillards
www.dillards.com/bridal/bridal.htm
1-800-626-6001

Home Depot
Registry available in stores but not online. Call your local store.

JCPenney
www.jcpenney.com
1-800-527-4438

Macy's
www.macysbridal.com/
1-888-989-9333

Pier 1 Imports
www.pier1.com/
1-800-245-4595

Sears Roebuck
www.sears.com/
Call your local store

TheGift.com
www.thegift.com

Registry service through the Internet

Wedding Network
www.weddingnetwork.com/
1-800-628-5113

Wedding Resorts and Chapels

All-inclusive wedding resorts

SuperClubs
www.superclubs.com/GeneralInfo/wed-FR.html
1-800-GO-SUPER

Sandals
www.sandals.com/general/entry-wedding.html
1-800-SANDALS

Swept Away
www.sweptaway.com/weddings.htm
1-800-545-7937

Beaches
www.beaches.com/weddings-mainframe.html
1-800-BEACHES

U.S. wedding chapels

Quick Wed
Database listing wedding chapels across the United States
www.quickwed.com

(The following wedding chapels are listed alphabetically by state.)

Mentone Wedding Chapel
Mentone, AL
www.virtualcities.com/ons/al/n/alnc601.htm
(256) 634-4181

Last Minute Weddings

Coastal Helicopters
Juneau, AK
www.coastalhelicopters.com
(907) 789-5600

Eureka Springs, Arkansas—Dubbed "Honeymoon Capitol of The South"—is host to many unique wedding chapels. Please check out the following site for listings.

www.eureka-usa.com/romance/index.shtml#wedding
Request brochure under "Free Info" in Eureka Springs Tourist Center Links.

Or call Eureka Springs Tourist Center at (501) 253-0505

Little Bell Wedding Chapel
Bellefonte, AR
www.yournet.com/littlebell/littlebell.html
(870)743-2355

Colorado River Wedding Chapel
Bullhead City, AZ
1-800-762-8489 or (520) 754-0010

Apacheland Weddings
Gold Canyon, AZ
(602) 288-0957

Wedding Chapel of Mesa
Mesa, AZ
1-800-626-2779

Sedona Weddings
Sedona, AZ
www.shewy.com/wedding/sedonawd/
1-800-551-0448 or (520) 284-1986

Weddings In Sedona
Sedona, AZ
www.weddingsinsedona.com
1-800-973-3762 or (520) 639-3311

Victoria's Bed & Breakfast
Tombstone, AZ
www.tombstone1880.com/vsbb/index.htm
1-800-952-8216 or (520) 457-3677

Catalina Island Weddings
Avalon, CA
www.catalina.com/catwed.html
(310)510-2367

Hitching Post Wedding Chapel
Big Bear Lake, CA
1-800-828-4433

Weddings By The Sea
Half Moon Bay, CA
www.weddingsbythesea.com
(650) 548-7316

Virtual Lake Tahoe Weddings & Honeymoons
www.virtualtahoe.com/Weddings/

South Lake Tahoe Chamber of Commerce
South Lake Tahoe, CA
(503) 541-5255

Weddings and Renewals in Yosemite National Park
Mariposa, CA
www.yosemite.net/~paris/
(209) 742-6633

A Bayside Wedding
Monterey Peninsula, CA
www.baysidewedding.com/
1-800-898-6933 or (408) 372-8997

A By-the-Sea Wedding
Monterey Peninsula, CA
www.whps.com/wedding/
(831) 375-1900

Last Minute Weddings

Weddings Aboard The River City Queen
Sacramento, CA
www.rivercityqueen.com
1-800-794-2628 or (916) 921-1111

Santa Barbara Weddings
Santa Barbara, CA
www.santabarbaraweddings.com/
(805) 963-3790

Yolo Shortline Railroad
Woodland, CA
1-800-942-6387 or (916) 666-9646

Rocky Mountain Weddings
Breckenridge, CO
www.mountainweddings.com/
1-888-686-9333 or (970) 468-8403

Romantic River Song Inn
Estes Park, CO
Special Events at Inn: Elopement Package, vow renewals, and snowshoe weddings.
www.virtualcities.com/ons/co/e/coe8801.htm
(970) 586-4666

Alpine Wedding Chapel
Winter Park, CO
http://rkymtnhi.com/chapel
1-800-525-6923

Chapel of Love
Eustis, FL
www.dipadee.com/chapeloflove/
1-800-202-3770 or 352-483-2171

Banana Bay Resorts
Key West, FL
www.paradisekeywest.com/banabay.html00
1-800-226-2621 or (305) 296-6925

Chapel by the Sea
Key West, FL
www.paradisekeywest.com/chapelkw.html
1-800-603-2088

Dial "M" for Matrimony
Key West, FL
http://floridakeys.net/dialm/
1-800-672-0385 or (305) 296-0071

Amore' Wedding Chapel
Saint Augustine, FL
www.amore.wedding.com
(904) 826-0715

Half Moon Beach Club
Sarasota, FL
http://halfmoon-lidokey.com/half2.html
1-800-358-3245 or (941) 388-3694

Walt Disney World
Orlando, FL
www.disney.com/DisneyWorld/MoreVacations/wed74.html
(407) 828-3400

Hawaii offers countless wedding service providers and coordinators to help you plan your wedding in paradise. In addition to the ones listed below, we recommend you visit or call:

Hawaii Better Business Bureau
(808) 536-6956

Hawaii State Tourism Site for Weddings
www.gohawaii.com/hokeo/wedding/planner.html

Hawaii Visitors Bureau
(808) 923-1811

1st Hawaiian Wedding and Bridal Directory
www.seewaikiki.com/bridal/

Last Minute Weddings

Maui Chamber of Commerce
www.mauichamber.com/
(808) 871-7711

Hawaii State Vacation Planner
www.hshawaii.com/
(Select your island and go to the link for weddings.)

Coconut Coast Weddings & Photography
Hanalei, HI
http://kauaiwedding.com
1-800-585-5595 or (808) 826-5557

Hanalei Bay Resort Weddings
Kauai, HI
http://hanaleibayresort.com/
1-800-827-4427 or (808) 826-6522

Hawaiian Romance
Kahului, Maui, HI
www.mauivows.com/
1-800-377-9745

Sunshine Helicopters
Kahului, HI
www.sunshinehelicopters.com
1-800-544-2520 or (808) 871-5600 x112

Hawaiian Island Weddings, Inc.
Kihei, Maui, HI
www.maui.net/~weddings
1-800-368-5502 or (808) 875-0350

A Dream Wedding Maui Style
Lahaina, Maui, HI
www.maui.net/~dreamwed/dream.html
1-800-743-2777 or (808) 661-1777

Romantic Maui Weddings
Lahaina, Maui, HI
www.justmauied.com
1-800-808-4144 or (808) 874-6444

Maui Weddings from the Heart
Kihei, Maui, HI
www.mauiwed.com
(808) 874-8755

Royal Hawaiian Weddings
Puunene, Maui, HI
1-800-659-1866 or (808) 875-8569

White Orchid Wedding
Wailuku, Maui, HI
www.maui.net/~awow
1-800-240-9336 or (808) 242-VOWS

A #1 Hawaii Weddings
www.lovehawaii.com
(808) 235-6966

Married In Madison County
Winterset, IA
1-800-841-5336 or (515) 462-3479

Colonial Wedding House
Coeur D'Alene, ID
www.cda-idaho.com/wedding/
1-800-482-5384 or (208) 664-8077

Hitching Post Wedding Chapel
Coeur D'Alene, ID
(208) 664-5510

Katie's Wild Rose Inn
Coeur D'Alene, ID
1-800-371-4545 or (208) 765-9474

Wilderness Weddings
McCall, ID
www.WildernessWeddings.com/
(208) 634-2053

Last Minute Weddings

Oldtown Wedding Chapel
Bloomingdale, IL
www.weddingchapel.com
(630) 539-2518

Brown County Weddings & The Wedding Loft Chapel
Nashville, IN
1-888-404-5683 or (812) 988-1892

New Orleans Wedding Chapel
New Orleans, LA
www.coastcasinos.com/chapel/index.html
1-888-365-7111 or (504) 949-0990

Chapel of Love
Located in Mall America
Bloomington, MN
www.chapeloflove.com
1-800-298-5683 or (612) 854-4656

Whitetail Ranch
Ovando, MT
www.whitetailranch.com
1-888-987-2624 or (406) 793-5627

Canyon Wedding Chapel
Red Lodge, MT
1-800-823-3681 or (406) 446-2681

Montana Whitewater
(Seasonal)
1-800-799-4465

Deacon's Beach Wedding Chapel
Mars Hill, NC
1-800-242-7359 or (828) 689-3893

Crestwood Bed and Breakfast
Ashuelot, NH
www.sover.net/~meg910
(603) 239-6393

Fairytale Weddings
Santa Fe, NM
www.santafe.org/fairytale/
(505) 438-7116

Enchanted Weddings of Taos
Taos, NM
www.newmex.com/wedding/
1-888-376-6325

The Falls Wedding Chapel
Niagara Falls, NY
www.businessvillage.com/wedding.html
1-888-311-8697 or (716) 285-5570

Wedding Chapel
Niagara Falls, NY
1-800-785-5683 or (716) 285-4929

Reno Weddings
For locations in Carson City, Reno/Sparks, Lake Tahoe and
Virginia City.
www.reno.net/wedding/

Vegas Wedding
www.vegas.com/weddings/chapels.html

Viva Las Vegas Themed Weddings
Las Vegas, NV
www.vivalasvegasweddings.com
1-800-574-4450 or (702) 384-0771

Mount Airy Lodge in the Poconos
Mount Pocono, PA
www.mountairylodge.com
1-888-568-2479 x7078 or 1-800-441-4410

The Charleston Chapel for Weddings
Charleston, SC
1-800-416-2779

Last Minute Weddings

A Wedding by the Sea
Hilton Head, SC
http://hhisc.com/weddings/
(843) 342-3981

**Pigeon Forge Department of Tourism Wedding
Information**
www.pigeon-forge.tn.us/wedding.html
1-800-251-9100

Gatlinburg Chamber of Commerce Wedding Site
www.gatlinburg.com/wedding1.htm
1-800-900-4148

Wedding Chapel of the Chattanooga Inc.
Chattanooga, TN
1-800-330-2322 or (423) 855-5728

Wedding Loft Wedding Chapel
Jonesborough, TN
1-800-845-0016 or (615) 384-0513

Wedding Chapel
Memphis, TN
1-800-755-9885 or (901) 755-9885

Town Square Wedding Chapel
Sevierville, TN
1-800-619-3397 or (423) 429-3397

Bridal Path Wedding Chapel
Springfield, TN
www.edge.net/bridalpath/bride3.htm
1-800-845-0016 or (615) 384-0513

Wedding Chapel, Inc.
Springfield, TN
1-800-845-0016 or (615) 384-0513

Heartland Little River Wedding Chapel
Townsend, TN
http://gsonet.com/heart/index.htm
1-800-448-8697 or (423) 448-9432

Lover's Lane Wedding Chapel
Dallas, TX
(214) 352-5232

24 Hour Wedding Chapel
Houston, TX
(713) 734-2525

Chapel of Love
Pasadena, TX
(713) 477-2316

Absolutely Anyone-Anywhere-Anytime Anykind of Wedding
Seattle, WA
www.weddingsido.com
(206) 624-3855

Chapel by the Sea, Inc.
Tacoma, WA
(253) 584-1338

Grand Teton Weddings
Jackson Hole, WY
www.jimedia.com/tetonweddings/
1-800-842-0391 or (307) 739-0395

Just Weddings of Jackson Hole
Jackson Hole, WY
1-800-982-6919

Online Resource Sites

Discount airfare sites

11th Hour Vacations
www.11thhourvacations.com/

Air Fare
www.airfare.com/

Cheap Fares
www.cheapfares.to/

Discount Airfare
www.discount-airfare.com/

Priceline
www.priceline.com

You Price It
www.youpriceit.com/

Wedding Web sites

Bride's Magazine
www.brides.com/

Elegant Bride
www.elegantbridemagazine.com

Modern Bride
www.modernbride.com/

Premier Bride
www.premierbride.com/

The Best Man
www.thebestman.com/

The Knot
www2.theknot.com/default.htm

The Wedding Channel
www.weddingchannel.com

Today's Bride
www.todaysbride.com/

Ultimate Internet Wedding Guide
www.ultimatewedding.com/

USA Bride Wedding Magazine
www.usabride.com/

Wed Net, The Wedding Network
www.wednet.com/

Wedding Bells
www.weddingbells.com/

Wedding Central
www.weddingcentral.com/

Wedding Details
www.weddingdetails.com/planning/

Wedding Line
www.weddingline.com/

Wedding Pages Online
www.weddingpages.com/

Wedding Spot
www.weddingspot.com

Wedding chat rooms/bulletin boards

Cyber-Bride
www.pvpvideo.com/chatnow.html

That Home Site
www.thathomesite.com/forums/wedding/

Ultimate Wedding Crafts Bulletin Board
www.wwvisions.com/craftbb/weddingcrafts.html

Ultimate Wedding Live Chat
www.ultimatewedding.com/chat.htm

Last Minute Weddings

Wedding Chat Room
www.shoponthenet.com/CustomCare/chatpage.htm

Wedding Planning Chat
weddingplanning.com/chat.html

Wedding.com Chat Room
www.wedding.com/chatwelcome.html

Weddinginfo Chat
www.weddinginfo.com/chat/INDEX.HTM

WhiteWedding.com Chat
www.whitewedding.com/slyleindex.html

Web wedding announcement sites*

I Thee Web
www.itheeweb.com

In Love
www.inlove.com

Our Big Day
www.ourbigday.com

Proud Parents
www.proudparents.com

The Wedding Helpline
www.weddinghelpline.com

Wedding Channel
www.weddingchannel.com
Click "Our Wedding"

Weddings on the Web
www.webwed.com

not all sites are free

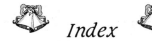

Index

Last Minute Weddings